Glenna
You have been a
blessing to my life.
I thank God for you and
your service to the Lord!
Patrick Meed
Ps 37:4

Lessons for the Life of Faith

Lessons for the Life of Faith

by Patrick Mead

ISBN: 978-0-557-05202-8

Library of Congress Control Number: 2009902054

This book is dedicated to

My Lord and Savior, Jesus Christ,
My wife Christy, and my three daughters, Abigail, Maribeth, and Caroline for their constant support of my calling and dreams,
John and Sue Hatcher for catching the vision of my ministry,
The First Baptist Church of Purcell, Oklahoma for allowing me to write and preach Lessons for the Life of Faith.

Contents

INTRODUCTION

While I grew up, I had the privilege of being the youngest of three sons. If you are the youngest of multiple siblings then you know some of the benefits that come with that position. Parents tend to spoil the youngest and they are often more lenient when it comes to discipline. Of course, now that I'm older that doesn't seem like a benefit, but at the time I thought it was. What was most advantageous in my development as an adult was that I was able to watch my older brothers and learn from their examples.

Having two older brothers gave me an idea of which choices I wanted to make and which ones I needed to avoid. As a child, I didn't realize that my brothers were examples for me. Unfortunately I didn't steer clear of all the mistakes they made, but I was careful, at all costs, to avoid at least some of their blunders. At the same time, I was careful to follow some of the fruitful choices they made. The most important decision I made based on one of my brother's examples was to accept Jesus Christ as my Lord and Savior. Had it not been for a sibling's godly example I may not have desired to follow Christ.

As Christians who live two millennia beyond the cross, we find ourselves in a privileged position. Contemporary believers, to some degree, are the younger brothers and sisters of those who have gone before us. In the same way I was able to learn from my earthly brothers, we Christians can learn from fellow saints who have gone before us.

The writer of Hebrews tells us, "Therefore, since we have so great a cloud of witnesses surrounding us, let us also lay aside every encumbrance and the sin which so easily entangles us" (Hebrews 12:1). In short, we are to learn from those who went before us so that we do not become so easily knotted up in our sin. When we look back to Hebrews 11, we see that the statement "by faith" introduces many of the names of the Old Testament saints.

Clearly, Abel, Noah, Moses, Rahab, and the others were men and women of faith. Were they perfect in their walk of faith? No! But they did remove the things that entangled them and they ran the race with endurance. The same is true of us. We will never live a perfect life of faith, but we can learn from others to hopefully avoid their costly mistakes and imitate their wise decisions.

Although each person mentioned in Hebrews 11 is important, the greatest example of living a life of is Abraham. Why is his life so essential to our understanding the life of faith? The New Testament is filled with references to him. Passages in Romans 4, Galatians 3, James 2, and Hebrews 11 attest to the fact that Abraham was a man of faith. You could easily declare that Abraham is *the* hero of faith found in the biblical records, for the writer of Hebrews 11 attributed more verses to Abraham than to any other person of faith mentioned in that exceptional chapter.[1]

Although Abraham is considered the hero of faith, he is in no way without his flaws. In fact, we can learn as much from his flaws as from his virtues.[2] As we observe Abraham's life, we'll notice his struggle to trust God, especially when times get tough. Every true believer faces conflicts and trials that test our ability to trust God; therefore, Abraham's life gives us much to glean from concerning our own pilgrimage.[3]

To learn how to live a life of faith, we will study Abraham as recorded in the first book of the Bible. The life of Abraham makes up approximately thirteen of the fifty chapters of Genesis. As we read through and study Abraham's life, we will learn more about who God is, how we should behave as Christians, and how, even when we fail, God is ever-faithful.

Our study will begin in Genesis 11 where we'll examine the origin of the life of faith—how it begins and what it entails.

---

[1]Bruce K. Waltke, *Genesis: A Commentary* (Grand Rapids: Zondervan, 2001) 192.
[2]Waltke 193.
[3]Waltke 195.

As we study Genesis 12, we'll learn about Abraham's faltering faith and we'll see that all Christians' faith falters at times due to a variety of circumstances, but despite our unfaithfulness, God is always faithful and He is able to bring us back to Him. Genesis 13 primarily deals with conflicts that Abraham experiences within his own family. We'll learn how to apply what God's Word teaches us so we can live in unity within the body of Christ.

Spiritual warfare is a part of every Christian's life, and it was no different with Abraham. Genesis 14 helps us to examine that spiritual people experience spiritual warfare, that we must be in the world, but not of it, and that God is the ultimate source of spiritual victory. As we move into Genesis 15, we are reminded of the hymn "Standing on the Promises of God." God's promises are many, they are supernatural, and God's character ensures that He is faithful to keep every promise.

As we move on to study Genesis 16, we'll learn about God's covenant promise to Abraham and Sarah—to give them a son in their old age. Yet despite God's supernatural promise, Abraham and Sarah react humanly to this divine promise, they attempt to take things into their own hands because waiting is difficult and we tend to look to worldly ways rather than to wait on God.

The emphasis in Genesis 17 is on the covenants of God, how He makes His covenants, reveals information about them according to His timing, and ultimately fulfills them. As we study this portion of Genesis, we'll get a greater picture of an almighty and powerful God, who provides His promises and blessings to us solely because of His goodness, not by anything that man does. Yet Abraham and Sarah forgot about God's divine power—his ability to do all things, even those we deem impossible. And we learn in Genesis 18 that nothing is too difficult for God.

As we continue in Genesis 18, we learn from Abraham's life of faith that he is an representative of God who has a great responsibility to be the light and salt in a dark and dying world.

So too, Christians are to be great preservatives in the sinful world in which we live.

When we study Genesis 19, we focus on the life of Abraham's nephew, Lot. We watch a righteous man's spiritual life decline and see its effect on his family and posterity. Through this study, we can learn from the negative examples of Lot and be convicted to live holier lives, separate from the world and its temptations, which can lead to a destructive demise.

We'll return to the study of Abraham's life and see how his life affected those around him. Unbelievers living in our midst notice our foolish and faithful ways. Our foolishness can destroy those around us, but as we'll study in Genesis 20, God can and does intervene and forgive. As we near the end of the chapters of Genesis that tell us about Abraham's journey of faith, we get a glimpse of Abraham's spiritual growth and how his life of faith led to one of obedience to God, yielding to the power of God so the Lord's will can be accomplished.

Further emphasis on how mature Christians can make a difference in our community is revealed in Genesis 21, where we see Abraham and a pagan king work together so that we can deliver the message of true peace to our neighbors. Finally, as we study Genesis 22, we'll learn in detail about the divine test of God when he tells Abraham to sacrifice his long-awaited son, Isaac. The ultimate maturity of Abraham's faith is revealed as we examine his reaction and behavior to God's request. And, we'll see the incredible mercy and power of our God through these passages of Scripture. From Genesis 11 through 22, God will reveal to us his purposes and power, and teach us through the lessons of one who went before us how to live a life of faith.

CHAPTER I:

THE GENESIS OF THE LIFE OF FAITH

Genesis 11:27–12:9

The Setting of the Life of Faith (Genesis 11:27–32)

The last six verses of Genesis 11 give us the background or setting for the life of faith and the life of Abraham. (Note that at this point in the narrative Abraham is still named Abram.) In these verses the author introduces us to three aspects of the setting of the life of faith, negative aspects that reveal how important it is to live a life of faith. Let's review the text.

> Now these are the records of the generations of Terah. Terah became the father of Abram, Nahor and Haran; and Haran became the father of Lot. And Haran died in the presence of his father Terah in the land of his birth, in Ur of the Chaldeans. And Abram and Nahor took wives for themselves. The name of Abram's wife was Sarai; and the name of Nahor's wife was Milcah, the daughter of Haran, the father of Milcah and Iscah. And Sarai

> was barren; she had no child. And Terah took Abram his son, and Lot the son of Haran, his grandson, and Sarai his daughter-in-law, his son Abram's wife; and they went out together from Ur of the Chaldeans in order to enter the land of Canaan; and they went as far as Haran, and settled there. And the days of Terah were two hundred and five years; and Terah died in Haran. (Genesis 11:27–32)

In these verses we see the setting of judgment, hopelessness, and worldliness, all of which are detrimental to life, all of which can be overcome only by a true life of faith.

Judgment

Though the text does not explicitly detail judgment, you can find it when you begin to understand the nature of the narrative. Moses, the author of the Pentateuch (the first five books of the Old Testament), records the call of Abram to a life of faith after the incident with the Tower of Babel (Genesis 11:1–9). In those first nine verses, God judges sinful man by confusing the language of the whole earth and scattering man over the face of the earth. By placing the call of Abram after the judgment of Babel, Moses gave us a picture of God's grace and salvation in the midst of judgment. This is parallel to the story of Noah where we have God's grace and salvation in the midst of a terrible flood, a flood that came as judgment upon sinners.[4]

The only way sinful man can escape the judgment of God is by living a life of faith in God's gift of salvation. What was true for Noah and Abraham is true for us. We are born into and live in a setting of judgment, which can be avoided only through faith by God's grace.

---

[4]John Sailhamer, *The Pentateuch as Narrative* (Grand Rapids: Zondervan, 1992) 139.

Hopelessness

The second aspect of the setting of the life of faith is that of hopelessness as revealed in Genesis 11:30, "Sarai was barren; she had no child." This verse describes the hopelessness that both Abram and Sarai experienced. In ancient times, barrenness was a major embarrassment, and it was believed to be a sign of God's judgment. Furthermore, it meant that the generational inheritance pattern would be disrupted, leaving no one to care for a couple in their old age.[5] One commentator described this verse as "an effective metaphor for hopelessness … [with] no human power to invent a future."[6]

Sarai thought she would not experience the greatest joy women longed for. For Abram there would be no descendants, leaving no sons to pass down the family inheritance. A great deal of hopelessness consumed the aged couple, but soon—very soon—a summons to a life of faith would change their hopelessness to hopefulness. Hope would be on the horizon, but only through a life of faith. God's gift of grace and salvation not only frees people from judgment, but also brings hope and a future to those who accept that generous gift through faith.

Worldliness

The final aspect of the setting of the life of faith is worldliness, which is revealed not only in the geographical location of Abram's family, but also in the names given to certain family members.

Genesis 11 tells us that Terah was Abram's father and Abram had two brothers, Nahor and Haran. Haran died before his father in the birthplace of all three brothers, the Ur of the

---

[5]John H. Walton and Victor H. Matthews, *The Bible Background Commentary* (Downers Grove: Intervarsity Press, 2000) 35.

[6]Walter Brueggemann, *Genesis: A Bible Commentary for Teaching and Preaching* (Atlanta: John Knox, 1982) 116.

Chaldeans. After Haran's death, Terah took his family and made his way toward Canaan, but he would not make it there, for we are told in Genesis 11:31 that Terah and his family "went as far as Haran, and settled there."

Knowing about the cities of Ur and Haran are significant to understanding the culture that Abram would be summoned from. Both cities were known for their pagan worship; the chief god of both cities was the moon god Sin.[7] Though the culture they lived in is not enough evidence to suggest that Terah and his family were at one time worshippers of the moon god Sin, it is highly likely that they were. We can reach this conclusion by considering the names of some of Terah's family members. Abram was married to Sarai, who was his half sister, most likely from a different wife. In the Hebrew language Sarai's name means "princess," but in the Akkadian language it means "queen," which is the name of the moon god's companion. Terah's son Nahor married his niece Milcah. Milcah's name is also another Akkadian term for "queen" and is the title of Ishatar, the moon god's daughter.[8]

When you weigh the cultural evidence as well as the substantiation found within the naming of family members, it is safe to conclude that Terah and his family were worldly in their practice. They had been pagan worshippers. Though the moon god was probably a prominent object of Abram's family worship, the likelihood that they worshipped many gods is high. This polytheistic people believed that these so-called gods revealed themselves through works of nature. To obtain favor with these false gods, worshippers would try to manipulate the gods by flattering and enticing them.[9]

Just like Abram we are born into a setting of judgment, hopelessness, and worldliness, where only God's gift of grace and salvation can bring deliverance. By hearing God's summons

---

[7]John E. Hartley, *Genesis* (Peabody: Hendrickson Publishers, 2000) 131.
[8]Hartley 131.
[9]Walton and Matthews 36.

to a life of faith and responding, we can be delivered; it is our only hope. And it was Abram's only hope; he heard the summons to a life of faith and he responded.

The Summons to a Life of Faith

What exactly does God's summons to a life of faith consist of? Genesis 12 answers this question for us in the first three verses. "Now the LORD said to Abram, 'Go forth from your country, and from your relatives and from your father's house, to the land which I will show you; and I will make you a great nation, and I will bless you, and make your name great; and so you shall be a blessing; and I will bless those who bless you, and the one who curses you I will curse. And in you all the families of the earth shall be blessed' " (Genesis 12:1–3). Packed into these three verses is the beginning of the story of the Lord summoning Abram to renew his faith in God, to relinquish all that is familiar in his life, and ultimately to receive inconceivable promises from the Lord.

A Summons to Renew

At first glance, it would seem that this is the first time Abram had heard the call of God upon his life, but several reasons lead us to believe that is not so. Genesis 12:1 begins, "Now the Lord said to Abram ..." God is renewing his call upon Abram's life, calling Abram to rededicate his life to the journey of faith that started years before. How do we know? Look back to Genesis 11:31. "Terah took Abram his son, and Lot the son of Haran, his grandson, and Sarai his daughter-in-law, his son Abram's wife; and they went out together from Ur of the Chaldeans in order to enter the land of Canaan." Now the Lord does not specifically speak to Terah or Abram in this text, but we can see God directing them to leave Ur to travel to Canaan, a clear indication that God is calling Terah and his family.[10]

Further evidence that Terah and Abram heard the summons to a life of faith in Ur is found in two other passages, one in the Old Testament and another in the New Testament. Genesis 15:7 reads, "And He [God] said to him, 'I am the Lord who brought you out of Ur of the Chaldeans, to give you this land to possess it.' " The Lord undoubtedly declares that his first summons upon Abram came about not while he was in Haran, but while he was in his birthplace, Ur of the Chaldeans. This truth is substantiated in Acts 7:2–4 when Stephen said, "Hear me, brethren and fathers! The God of glory appeared to our father Abraham when he was in Mesopotamia, before he lived in Haran, and said to him, 'Depart from your country and your relatives, and come into the land that I will show you.' Then he departed from the land of the Chaldeans, and settled in Haran. And from there, after his father died, God removed him into this country in which you are now living." We find more evidence that Genesis 12:1 is a summons to renew in the tense of the verb "said." The tense is past perfect, which suggests this is not the first time God has spoken, but it is a reminder that he has already spoken to Abram and is now calling Abram to renew his commitment to a life of faith.[11]

Even Abram at first had a hard time believing God. Abram heard the call of God while he was in Ur but, like his father, he was willing to settle in Haran until he heard the summons to renew. The truth we gain from this is that the life of faith is a process. That is, when we begin the journey, our ability to trust in God is not perfect. In fact, the journey of faith is really a journey of maturity. We will see that Abram's life of faith matured over the years because a life of faith is ongoing. Likewise when you and I start the journey of faith, it is a process of maturity. And just as Abram had his moments of struggling to

---

[10]Walton and Matthews 131.
[11]Waltke 204.

trust God, so do we. Just as Abram wanted to hold on to the comfortable and worldly, so do we. During moments when we are struggling to trust God and holding on to worldly comforts, we need to hear the summons to renew once again—to remind us that God has something better for us than what the world has to offer.

As Abram received a summons to renew, so also did others. Another biblical example is Abram's father. We can only speculate what Terah heard from the Lord, but we do know that he set out with his family to go to Canaan. Whatever the circumstances, it is safe to say that Terah never made it to Canaan; instead he settled for what life had to offer in Haran. It is possible that Terah started a life of faith, but became a castaway. Perhaps he was no longer useful to the world because he wanted to hold on to worldly ways, while still wanting God's blessings upon his life. The tale of Terah is like the story of many of God's people who start the journey of faith well, but somewhere down the road settle for what the world offers and fail to enjoy the blessings of God that come upon a life of faith.

Several years ago, while working on my undergraduate degree, I had the opportunity to spend three weeks at the Stephen Olford Center for Biblical Preaching for their summer institute. One of the greatest joys was meeting and spending time with Stephen Olford. While there, Dr. Olford told us of a time in his life when he was holding on to the comfortable and the worldly. He was drifting away from Christ and was spending his time racing motorcycles. One winter night Dr. Olford had a motorcycle accident. His doctors told him that he had only weeks to live. While he was in the hospital, his father, Fredrick Olford, who was a missionary in Africa, sent him a letter that read, "Only one life it soon shall pass, only what is done for Christ will last." The Lord gave Dr. Olford a summons to renew his life. As a result, he would go on to become one of the greatest preachers ever to live.

The summons to renew is also a summons to relinquish. If Abram were going to enjoy the blessings of God, he would have to relinquish the comfortable and the worldly and follow the Lord. The remainder of Genesis 12:1 reveals that this summons to a life of faith was and is a summons to relinquish the things that can hinder the journey.

A Summons to Relinquish

The summons given to Abram is stated simply "go forth." The imperative verb means "to go out." The Hebrew imperative emphasizes that the subject needs to leave, "You [Abram] go forth."[12] The picture this command gives is one of leaving and relinquishing. One person has said that the Hebrew verb "lek-leka," which we translate "go forth," is a Hebrew expression that has the idea of one "determinedly disassociating oneself."[13] Abram is commanded, by God's great determination, to disassociate himself and to relinquish things that he may put his trust in, so that he can instead trust in the Lord.

Three prepositional phrases describe the things that Abram must relinquish if he is going to continue the journey of the life of faith: "Go forth *from your country*, and *from your relatives*, and *from your father's house*, to the land which I will show you" (emphasis added). What is the significance of the things that God commanded Abram to relinquish? What exactly was the Lord asking Abram to give up?

The Lord was asking Abram to give up his past and present situation to trust the Lord to give him hope and a future. In a sense, the Lord was asking Abram to give up the things that may hinder his progress in the journey of faith.

You can understand the significance of the Lord asking Abram to leave his country only by understanding the country itself. I remind you that the call of Abram came while he was in Ur of the Chaldeans. Scholars believe that Ur was a prosperous port city that flourished because of the great deal of trade that

---

[12]*The NET Bible*, (Biblical Studies Press, L.L.C.: 1996) 51.
[13]Waltke 205.

took place along the coastal waterways. Two great rivers, the Euphrates and the Tigris, made their home in Ur. The rich soil produced corn, date-palm crops, apples, grapes, pomegranates, and tamarisks.[14] Canaan did not compare to the luxurious comforts of Ur, yet the Lord was asking Abram to relinquish his land's riches.

Abram was also commanded to leave his people and his relatives. The Lord commanded Abram to move to a different place and a different culture where the people may be his enemies. This command is like asking an American to leave the comforts of America and go live with terrorists across the globe. When Abram lived among his own people he found acceptance, affluence, and protection, but now the Lord told him to leave it all behind.[15]

Not only was Abram to leave the comforts of his country and culture, but also he was to leave the blessings and brotherhood of his clan. Abram was to leave all of his immediate family. To leave his father's house meant that Abram would have to relinquish his identity (for the ancient world identified people with their household) and his inheritance.[16] Had Abram and his family been able to move as a clan, there would have been a small group to lend support and protection in a new country and a new culture. But God commanded Abram to leave his immediate family behind.[17]

This seems harsh when we look at all that God was asking Abram to surrender, but God knows what is best when it comes to the journey of faith, and he knows what is best for our spiritual development and progress in our life of faith. For Abram and all his people throughout the ages, God has consistently called us to

---

[14]James Montgomery Boice, *Genesis, An Expositional Commentary*, vol. 2 (Grand Rapids: Baker, 1982) 439–40.
[15]Boice 440.
[16]Walton and Matthews 35.
[17]Walton and Matthews 440.

leave the things in which we find safety and security, and place our total trust in him.

Throughout the Bible we see that God consistently gives his followers this summons to relinquish. Our Lord Jesus said the same thing in a different way, "If anyone wishes to come after me, he must deny himself, and take up his cross daily and follow me" (Matthew 16:24). The summons to a life of faith is always a summons to relinquish—to relinquish a life of judgment, a life of hopelessness, and a life of worldliness. The summons to a life of faith is a summons to a total commitment to the Lord.

I am reminded of an anecdote of the chicken and the pig. The pig asked the chicken, "What shall we have for breakfast?" "Let's have ham and eggs," replied the chicken. The pig said, "Oh no, not ham." "Why not," said the chicken, "I will supply the eggs and you supply the ham." The pig then responded, "For you it only means involvement, but for me it will take total commitment."[18] In the same way the summons to a life of faith is not a summons to involvement, but a summons to complete commitment.

The summons to a life of faith means we must give up everything temporal in which we take refuge, and instead trust the Lord to be our security and safety, our protection and prosperity.

But so many times when people hear the summons to a life of faith they focus only on the fact that the Lord calls them to relinquish everything to follow him. They fail to see that blessings will come from letting go. Even the disciples had a hard time with the summons to relinquish, demonstrated after Jesus' encounter with the Rich Young Ruler. After Jesus said, "It is easier for a camel to go through the eye of the needle than for a rich man to enter the kingdom of God," Peter responded by saying, "Behold we have left our homes and followed you." Jesus

---

[18]Roy B. Zuck, *The Speaker's Quote Book* (Grand Rapids: Kregel, 1997) 78.

assured Peter that though he relinquished everything to follow him, he would receive a greater blessing to come.[19]

What many people fail to understand is that when we relinquish all to follow the Lord, we receive the greatest blessings in return—blessings that do not compare to the things we give up. Abram's summons to relinquish was also a summons to receive.

A Summons to Receive

Abram was to leave his country, his culture, and his clan and go "to the land which I [God] will show you …" This would require a great deal of faith and trust from Abram, but God would not leave him oblivious to what he would do for Abram. In Genesis 12:2–3 the Lord told Abram what he would receive when he complied with the command to "go forth." In these verses we see seven statements or promises of God in response to Abram's obedience to the life of faith. God pledged to Abram, "And I will make you a great nation, and I will bless you, and make your name great; and so you shall be a blessing; and I will bless those who bless you, and the one who curses you I will curse and in you all the families of the earth will be blessed" (Genesis 12:2–3).

It is important to note a few things about these seven statements before we understand the significance of the statements. First, we should not overlook the number of promises that the Lord gave Abram. In the Bible, the number seven often connotes "completeness" or "wholeness." The implication is that when you start the journey of faith, you start the process of becoming complete and whole as God intended for his creation.

Second, the word "bless" appears five times in Genesis 12:2–3. The word "bless" appears only five times in the first eleven chapters of Genesis.[20] By using "bless" five times in only two verses, scholars believe that Moses is linking the promises

[19]Luke 18:18–30.
[20]Waltke 205.

given to Abram with the creation account, thus confirming that Abraham is of the seed of the woman referred to in chapter 3, verse 15 of Genesis.[21] You can see that Abraham is a key figure in God's unfolding plan of redemption. Furthermore, God's blessing of redemption always brings a power to live life the way God intended; it enhances life and brings about the increase of life.[22]

The promise of blessings can be put into two categories: the first four blessings are fulfilled in the context of God making Abram a "great nation." The last three blessings are fulfilled in the context of God enabling Abram to become an instrument so that "all the families of the earth will be blessed."[23]

The first four promises can be considered God's promise of provision for Abram. In these God would provide Abram with hope and a future, with divine favor, and with character and success. The provision of hope is found in the Lord's promise to Abram, "I will make you a great nation." How would God make Abram into a great nation when Abram's wife Sarai was barren? It takes descendants to start a great nation, and Abram did not have any to offer. The provision of hope is a promise to Abram that relinquishing all would bring about a hope and a future. Sarai longed for a child; she could now be hopeful instead of hopeless.

The provision of divine favor is found in the Lord's statement, "I will bless you." This promise of provision is not specific as are the preceding and following promises. God will bless Abram both spiritually and physically. This blessing would be realized in the gift of fertility and fame.[24] This promise is one of personal blessing, a blessing that would bring richness upon

---

[21]Waltke 203.
[22]Waltke 205.
[23]Waltke 203.
[24]Allen P. Ross, Creation and Blessing: A Guide to the Study and Exposition of Genesis (Grand Rapids: Baker, 1996) 263.

Abram's life. God would prosper Abram in his family, in his business, and ultimately in his faith.[25]

The provision of fame and character is found in the Lord's statement, "and make your name great." The Lord's purpose here is to contrast humanity's statement in Genesis 11:4 at the Tower of Babel, "Come, let us build for ourselves a city, and a tower whose top will reach into heaven, and let us make for ourselves a name." Humans strive to make a name and become successful on their own, but true success is found only in a life of faith by trusting in and following the Lord. The idea of a great name goes beyond fame. In ancient times a great name was a "revelation of character." A great name referred to one who had "superior character."[26] A life of faith produces a life of righteous character, a character that can find its source only in God.

The final promise of provision that will be fulfilled in the promise of Abram becoming "a great nation," is "you shall be a blessing." It is difficult to understand because the verb is a Qal imperative. Is this a promise or a command? I contend that for practical purposes it is both. The grammar suggests that the verb form in this promise is a command that subordinates to the command for Abram to "go forth." Therefore this promise is one of purpose or consequence. As Abram obeys the Lord by relinquishing everything, he will then be a blessing for all to see. He would become an example of a life blessed of God. The implication of this promise of purpose goes beyond just being an example. We should not negate the imperative force of the verb in this promise. If God were going to bless all the families of the earth, then Abram and his descendants would have to be the message bearers to the rest of the world. Thus, being blessed by God has its responsibility of letting the rest of the world know about God's blessings.[27] This promise of purpose comes to a climax in the seventh promise.

---

[25]Boice 447.
[26]Waltke 205.
[27]Ross 263.

The last three promises fall into two categories: the promise of protection and the promise of purpose. Both of these promises are fulfilled in the fact that "all the families of the earth will be blessed" through God's blessing Abram.

The promise of protection is found in the Lord's statement in Genesis 12:3, "And I will bless those who bless you, and the one who curses you I will curse." This promise for Abram is a promise of God's protection as he made his journey of faith. This promise is significant when you realize that the Lord was asking Abram to leave the security and safety of his country, of his culture, and of his clan, and go to a place of uncertainty and hostility. God is promising Abram that though he is relinquishing what seems to be safety and security, true protection is found in the Lord. Those who would bless Abram in his journey of faith would be enriched, but those who hindered and became an enemy of Abram would be cursed.[28] You have only to observe the life of Abram as well as the life of Israel to see that the Lord has been faithful to fulfill this promise.

The promise of purpose is the seventh and final promise, "And in you all the families of the earth will be blessed." This seventh and final promise of blessing brings this great passage of promises given to Abram to a climactic end. The ultimate purpose of God calling Abram to a life of faith and blessing him with so many blessings is summed up in the great promise. God was calling Abram from a life of judgment, a life of hopelessness, and a life of worldliness, so Abram would be an example of God's divine blessings to the world. Ultimately, though, God was calling Abram to a life of faith so that through him the whole world would be blessed with the same summons to a life of faith as Abram. How would the Lord bless all the families of the earth through Abram?

The promise God gave in this climactic ending is a promise that is fulfilled in the person of Jesus Christ. The Lord summoned Abram to a life of faith and blessed him for a purpose,

---

[28]Ross 263.

that Abram may be the blessing-bearer to the entire world. From Abram would come the Messiah not only for the Jews, but also for the whole world. It is through Christ that we are truly saved from the setting of judgment, hopelessness, and worldliness.

The promise of purpose is in some sense a promise of responsibility. When God blesses, his blessings come with a great responsibility. Abram and his descendants, the people of Israel, would have the responsibility of communicating the truth of the Lord to the Gentile nations.

In the same way, we who are spiritual heirs of Abram through faith in Christ have the same responsibility. The Lord Jesus communicated this responsibility in this way, "Go therefore and make disciples of all the nations, baptizing them in the name of the Father and the Son and the Holy Spirit, teaching them to observe all that I commanded you; and lo, I am with you always, even to the end of the age."[29] The Great Commission, as we call it, is really the Great Recommission. God summons people to a life of faith and blesses them with salvation and eternal life, but with that blessing comes a responsibility. God's people are to communicate the blessings of salvation and life to those who find themselves in the setting of judgment, hopelessness, and worldliness. This is true for Abram according to this promise of purpose, and it is also true of the church.

The Lord's summons to relinquish is always a summons to receive. Just as Abram was promised the blessings of provision, protection, and purpose; so are we who have been summoned to a life of faith on this side of the cross. When we leave all to follow Christ, we can be assured that God will provide, God will protect, and that God has given us a purpose. The greatest promise that we have when we follow Christ is that God will provide us forgiveness of sins, salvation, and eternal life. But he also will provide for our daily needs as we make our way to our heavenly home. For all the promises of God are answered in the person of Jesus Christ. And we who are blessed

[29]Matthew 28:19–20.

by the life of faith have the responsibility of communicating our blessings from God to others.

You cannot help but wonder at the great promises that the Lord gave to Abram. But as great as the promises are, they would mean nothing apart from Abram's proper response to the summons to a life of faith. If Abram were going to enjoy the blessings of God and pass those blessings on, he would have to respond to the summons to a life of faith, and that he did. In his response to the summons to the life of faith Abram gives us a picture of what a life of faith looks like. Abram reveals in Genesis 12:4–9 the substance of a life of faith.

The Substance of a Life of Faith

> So Abram went forth as the LORD had spoken to him; and Lot went with him. Now Abram was seventy-five years old when he departed from Haran. And Abram took Sarai his wife and Lot his nephew, and all their possessions which they had accumulated, and the persons which they had acquired in Haran, and they set out for the land of Canaan; thus they came to the land of Canaan. And Abram passed through the land as far as the site of Shechem, to the oak of Moreh. Now the Canaanite was then in the land. And the LORD appeared to Abram and said, "To your descendants I will give this land." So he built an altar there to the LORD who had appeared to him. Then he proceeded from there to the mountain on the east of Bethel, and pitched his tent, with Bethel on the west and Ai on the east; and there he built an altar to the LORD and called upon the name of the LORD. And Abram journeyed on, continuing toward the Negev. (Genesis 12:4–9)

A key theme found in these six verses is the theme of Abram's obedience or compliance with the word of God. The heart of the life of faith is obedience. In the Bible "faith" and "obedience" are synonymous terms. Biblical faith is not a mere adherence to a set of beliefs. Biblical faith obeys and complies with the word of the Lord. Abram reveals this key theme in his response to God's command by complying with the word of the Lord.

The Substance of Compliance

Abram's compliance is first stated in verse 4: "So Abram went forth as the LORD had spoken to him." The verb "went forth" corresponds with the verb "go forth" in verse 1 of this same chapter. Again we see Abram's compliance stated in verse 5: "They set out for the land of Canaan; thus they came to the land of Canaan." To further emphasize Abram's compliance, verse 4 says, "So Abram went forth as the LORD had spoken to him." This was not a natural migration on Abram's part. He did not get up one morning and decide to go to Canaan. Rather, through obedience, he responded to the word of the Lord. This is significant because all obedience in the life of faith is compliance with the word of the Lord.[30]

The late Danish theologian and philosopher Soren Kierkegaard stressed the significance of "the personal experience of faith" and the importance of commitment and obedience in truly knowing God.[31] In teaching the importance of commitment and obedience in truly knowing God, he created a parable that he called *The Domestic Goose*.

In the parable Kierkegaard told of a flock of geese that lived in a barnyard. Every Sunday the flock of geese would gather together under the shade and listen as one gander preached of the glorious hope and destiny of the goose. The great goose

---

[30]Ross 264.

[31]Alister E. McGrath, *The Blackwell Encyclopedia of Modern Christian Thought* (Oxford: Blackwell, 1993) 300–301.

would proclaim and remind the geese of their purpose—namely flying. Each week they would hear the messages of flying and soaring high above the earth. But each week, instead of putting the great message of flying into practice, the geese would return to the barnyard to their daily routine of eating. At Christmastime the now plump and delicious geese were eaten. They never knew the joy of ascending into the blue skies and soaring in the clouds. Why would they never know the joy of flying? Kierkegaard's contention and the point of the parable is the lack of commitment and obedience to the message of flying.[32]

We must respond to the summons to a life of faith with compliance and obedience. So many people hear the summons to the life of faith Sunday after Sunday, only to go back to the barnyard and eat, never knowing the blessings that God has promised to those who follow him. Abram would do more than just listen; he would put the Lord's word into action by doing as the Lord commanded.

Does your life demonstrate the substance of obedience? Do you do more than just listen to the word of the Lord? Do you comply with the words of the Lord and put them into practice? The kind of faith that pleases the Lord goes beyond just a belief that God exists. In fact the writer of Hebrews put it this way, "And without faith it is impossible to please Him, for he who comes to God must believe that He is and that he is a rewarder of those who seek him" (Hebrews 11:6). In the same manner as Abram, we must not only believe that God exists, but we must also believe that God blesses the life of those who step out in obedience to his Word.

The primary theme and the key substance to the life of faith is obedience, but there are other things revealed in these verses that show us the substance of a life of faith. Another significant principle is that the life of faith will bring about conflict.

---

[32]James E. Hightower, Jr., *Illustrating the Gospel of Matthew* (Nashville: Broadman, 1992) 91–92.

The Substance of Conflict

When you start the journey of faith and desire to live the life of faith on a daily basis, you will experience conflict. What I mean by conflict is that you will come to many obstacles. Sarai's barren womb gives us one obvious example of an obstacle to the life of faith. Of course, Abram, not knowing how God would bring it about, trusted the Lord to provide him with a child. Each believer will face struggles and conflicts. Those of us on the journey of faith will find ourselves at times struggling to trust in God in hopeless situations. We become paralyzed and fail to move in obedience to God's command. But we must learn from Abram—when seemingly insurmountable conflicts arise, we must believe in the promises of God and trust fully in him.

We find another obstacle in verse 6, "Abram passed through the land as far as the site of Shechem, to the oak of Moreh. Now the Canaanite was then in the Land." The Hebrew word "moreh" means "teacher." Scholars believe that this was a place where pagan shrines were assembled and pagan teachings were proclaimed. The oak of Moreh indicates that the Lord was sending Abram to a culture where pagan teachings and ideas were handed down.[33] The statement, "Now the Canaanite was then in the Land" provides further evidence of a pagan culture. This culture would become a constant conflict to the life of faith.

Abram was commanded to go to the Land of Promise and he complied, but this journey of faith would not be without its conflict. Abram would find himself in a land filled with antagonists. The Canaanites were constant adversaries to Abram and his descendants. Furthermore, the pagan worship of the Canaanites would become a constant temptation for the people of Israel.[34] This summons to the life of faith and the blessings of the life of faith would not come without difficulties.

---

[33]Ross 266.
[34]Ross 266.

In the same manner, as we make our journey of faith to the "heavenly city" we too will find many stumbling blocks to our progress in and continuation of the life of faith. The obstacles will come from within and from without. Those that come from without come from a world that is antagonistic toward the things of the Lord. The world around us will do all it can to lay hurdles in our path, ones that appeal to the lust of the flesh, the lust of the eyes, and to the pride of life.

One of my favorite books is the allegory *Pilgrim's Progress*. Its main character, Christian, is making his way to the Celestial City. But to get to the Celestial City, Christian and his companions must go through the town of Vanity. In the city of Vanity is a fair that goes on every day and all hours. Those who are not careful walking through Vanity Fair can be sidetracked in their journey.

The world that we live in is a constant Vanity Fair. As Christians we have to pass through Vanity Fair, but we must be careful not to be sidetracked by it. We must avoid the obstacles to the life of faith. And this we can be sure of, a true life of faith will bring us face to face with conflict.

The Substance of Communication

The substance of communication takes place on the part of both God and man. In verses 7 through 8 we have God communicating his confirmation of his promises and his reward in response to Abram's obedience. We also find Abram communicating his faith and God's blessings to the dying world around him.

In verse 7 we see the Lord communicating his confirmation and reward upon Abram. "The Lord appeared to Abram and said, 'To your descendents I will give this land.' " Scholars believe that the appearing of the Lord to Abram in this verse is a visible appearing, thus making this what is called a theophany, an appearing of the pre-incarnate Christ. In his appearance to Abram, the Lord declares his pleasure with

Abram's obedience and confirms his promise to give him the land. It is interesting to compare the Lord's statement in verse 1, "to the land which I will show you," with the statement here in verse 7, "to your descendants I will give this land." When Abram complied, the Lord communicated his confirmation of the promise.

We see two aspects of Abram communicating his faith and God's blessing to those around him: his walk and his worship. By the way Abram lived his life, he seems to have influenced others to take this journey of faith with him. We see this truth revealed in verse 4, "Now Abram went forth as the Lord had spoken to him; and Lot went with him." Some have suggested that Lot's going with him was disobedience on Abram's part because he was to leave his father's household and go the Land of Promise. However, that should not be the conclusion of this statement. The text suggests that Lot went with his uncle voluntarily. It is safe to conclude that Abram's life of faith had such an influence on Lot that Lot himself was willing to leave it all and follow Abram and the Lord.

The substance of true faith communicates to those around us the hope that is found in the Lord, and it influences those we come in contact with. I am a Christian today because one of my older brothers communicated his life of faith to me by the way he lived his life. A believer communicates true faith by the way in which he lives.

We also see Abram communicating his faith and God's blessing through worship. In verses 7 and 8 it is recorded twice that Abram built an altar and worshipped the Lord. The significance of Abram building altars goes beyond the act of worship and truly moves to the act of witnessing. The altar was built for sacrificial worship. It was common in the pagan religions to have an altar for sacrifices. Building an altar communicated gratitude and devotion, thankfulness and consecration to the Lord.

Abram's response to the Lord's communication of confirmation of promise and reward in the first part of verse 7 was one of gratitude and devotion. But it was also a declaration and proclamation to those around him of the goodness and mercy of God. The building of altars was also a means of introducing the worship of a god in a new land.[35] But Abram was not introducing the worship of a new god. Instead he made known the only true God to a pagan nation that was steeped in judgment, hopelessness, and worldliness. The altars that Abram built were flags that he stuck in the ground to claim the land for the Lord and proclaim God's name.

In fact, what Abram did was to fulfill his responsibility of communicating the blessings of God to a dying world around him. Yes, the Lord was going to bless him, but with that blessing came a responsibility, to proclaim the name of the Lord to the ends of the earth. We see this taking place at the second altar that Abram built, "Then he proceeded from there to the mountain on the east of Bethel, and pitched his tent, with Bethel on the west and Ai on the east; and he built an altar to the Lord and called upon the name of the Lord." Abram built an altar and he "called upon the name of the Lord."

The expression "called upon the name of the Lord" is used in Genesis 4:26 and has the meaning of public proclamation of faith in the one true God. It refers to expressing one faith through prayer and praise. Martin Luther went as far as translating this phrase, "preached the name of the Lord."[36] Abram stuck a flag in the ground and started preaching the name of the Lord to those around him.

True faith must communicate to others the grace and mercy of God. The Lord told Abram in verse 2 that he would make his "name great" or "famous," and Abram's response was to make the Lord's name famous to all around him. The substance of a life of faith is communication, both on the part of God and man. God communicates his favor upon a life of faith, and people who live a life of faith have the responsibility of

---

[35]Walton and Matthews 36.
[36]Ross 267.

communicating their faith and the blessings of God through their walk and their worship, through their practice and their proclamation.

Every child of God must communicate to others the blessings and hope that are found in Christ. Charles Spurgeon communicated this need very well, "Having joined the church of God, are you content to let those around you sink to hell? What! Never tell of Christ's love? What! Never speak of salvation to your own children? Can this be right? In God's name wake up! What are you left on this earth for? If there is nothing for you to do, why are you in this sinful world?"[37] The Lord has blessed us through faith in his Son and we must in turn communicate that blessing to others.

The Substance of Continuation

The fourth and final observation concerning the substance of a life of faith is that of continuation. That is, a life of faith is one that perseveres and continues the journey of faith. This is what we see in verse 9, "Abram journeyed on, continuing toward the Negev." The Hebrew verb that we translate "journeyed" literally means to "pull up the tent and move to another place."[38] The picture that the verb communicates is a journey that continues to take place and this journey takes place in stages.

The continuous aspect of Abram's journey of faith should characterize every journey of faith. This continuous aspect is important when you realize that Abram had not received most of the blessings that God would provide. In fact, many of the blessings that God promised to Abram, Abram himself would not see fulfilled, but his descendants would. The writer of Hebrews declares that Abram and those men and women of faith like him "died in faith, without receiving the promises, but having seen

---

[37]Tom Carter, *2200 Quotations from the Writings of Charles H. Spurgeon* (Grand Rapids: Baker, 1998) 220.
[38]*The NET Bible* 52.

them and having welcomed them from a distance." Despite this, Abram continued to trust the Lord day by day to take care of him. Abram patiently made his journey of faith as he waited for the Lord to act on his promises, some of which were at a distance. What kept Abram going? Abram had a greater vision, not of an earthly city, but a vision of a heavenly city "whose architect and builder is God" (Hebrews 11:10).

The substance of continuation on the part of the life of faith finds its source in patience and submission, patience in the will and timing of God and submission to the sovereignty of God. Those who understand that "He who is faithful in a very little thing is faithful also in much" cultivate the substance of continuation (Luke 16:10).

Another aspect that helps God's people in the journey of faith is understanding that the journey takes place in stages. As we study the life of Abram, we will notice the many stages of his journey of faith. Abram's journey is represented by stages of failure and well as stages of success. There are times in Abram's journey where he fails to trust God and takes things in his own hands. Other times God asks Abram to do something great and he responds with enormous trust in God's ability to take care of him.

What stage do you find yourself in? For some of you the journey has not begun because you have never responded to the summons to a life of faith. Others of you have started the journey, but somewhere along the road you have been sidetracked. For still others you are right where you need to be and God is stretching you and maturing you in ways you never experienced before. You keep trusting, for the Lord will provide your every need.

One of the most influential men in my life and ministry is a man named David Hamilton. I met David while serving at First Baptist Church of Dallas. David was the right-hand man of Dr. O.S. Hawkins, a working relationship that started in Ada, Oklahoma and lasted some twenty years. When David came on staff at First Baptist something started to take place that would change his life forever. His vision started going bad and he was having terrible headaches. It was soon after these symptoms appeared that the doctors found a baseball-sized tumor in the middle of his brain. Doctors were not giving him much hope concerning surgery. If he made it through surgery it was highly likely that he would be in a vegetative state for the rest of his life. There was a slim ray of hope that he would live and that he would be able to function with some sense of normalcy. David made it through the surgery. His vision will never be the same and his speech was affected, but God pulled him through.

Because David's eyes were never the same he could not drive, so I had the responsibility of driving David to visit hospitals, nursing homes, and shut-ins. One day as he and I were talking about his surgery and condition I asked him how he was able to make it through such trying times. His answer was short and simple, "You look up to Jesus, for Jesus is always faithful to his promises." That is what kept him going in this stage of his journey, the faithfulness of a loving Savior. Though at times we are unfaithful to God, we can always be assured that God will be faithful to his promises.

CHAPTER II:

HOW TO KEEP YOUR FAITH FROM FALTERING

Genesis 12:10–13:4

Introduction

One of my favorite hymn writers is Fanny Crosby. Though she was blind, Fanny Crosby wrote over eight thousand hymns. I love the story of how she came to write the hymn *All the Way My Savior Leads Me*. Apparently, Fanny was worried because she needed five dollars to pay her bills. She had no idea where she would get the money. Fear consumed her. One day, while stressing over her predicament, she heard a knock at the door. Whoever it was had no idea of her need, but felt led to give Fanny exactly five dollars. Fanny, considered this experience a rebuke to her lack of trust, and she wrote these lyrics of her loving Guide:

> All the way my Savior leads me,
> Cheers each winding path I tread,
> Gives me grace for every trial,
> Feeds me with the living bread.
> Though my weary steps may falter,

And my soul athirst may be,
Gushing from the Rock before me,
Lo! a spring of joy I see,
Gushing from the Rock before me,
Lo! a spring of joy I see.

Fanny Crosby's faith faltered, we'll soon see that Abram's faith faltered, and inevitably in our own journey of faith we too will live through periods when our *weary steps may falter*.

As we study Abraham to learn lessons for the life of faith, we want to recognize the attitudes and choices that can encumber our journey. The journey is a process—with steps that lead to maturity—those of grand success and others of vast defeat. But our faithful God uses both successes and failures to mature us in our faith.

We already noted that though Abram started his journey of faith in Ur, he was sidetracked, and he and his father Terah settled in Haran. There Abram heard the summons to renew—the summons of a second chance—and he responded in faith and continued on his journey until he made it to Canaan.

As we study the next passages in Genesis, we find Abram in Canaan, the place where God wanted him to go. You could say that Abram is now in the center of God's will, but as we will see, trying circumstances will test Abram's faith. His faith will falter and he'll crash. But the collision will not be terminal, for God, in his faithfulness, will use Abram's failure to bless him and grow him in his life of faith. From Abram's example in this passage, we can learn how to keep our own faith from faltering when we face difficulties, and remember that our faith matures through challenging circumstances.

> Now there was a famine in the land; so Abram went down to Egypt to sojourn there, for the famine was severe in the land. It came about when he came near to Egypt, that he said to Sarai his wife, "See now, I know that you are a beautiful

woman; and when the Egyptians see you, they will say, 'This is his wife'; and they will kill me, but they will let you live. Please say that you are my sister so that it may go well with me because of you, and that I may live on account of you." It came about when Abram came into Egypt, the Egyptians saw that the woman was very beautiful. Pharaoh's officials saw her and praised her to Pharaoh; and the woman was taken into Pharaoh's house. Therefore he treated Abram well for her sake; and gave him sheep and oxen and donkeys and male and female servants and female donkeys and camels. But the LORD struck Pharaoh and his house with great plagues because of Sarai, Abram's wife. Then Pharaoh called Abram and said, "What is this you have done to me? Why did you not tell me that she was your wife? Why did you say, 'She is my sister,' so that I took her for my wife? Now then, here is your wife, take her and go." Pharaoh commanded his men concerning him; and they escorted him away, with his wife and all that belonged to him. So Abram went up from Egypt to the Negev, he and his wife and all that belonged to him, and Lot with him. Now Abram was very rich in livestock, in silver and in gold. He went on his journeys from the Negev as far as Bethel, to the place where his tent had been at the beginning, between Bethel and Ai, to the place of the altar which he had made there formerly; and there Abram called on the name of the LORD. (Genesis 12:10–13:4)

The Challenging Circumstance

> Now there was a famine in the land; so Abram went down to Egypt to sojourn there, for the famine was severe in the land. (Genesis 12:10)

Abram's challenging circumstance involved hunger. Verse 10 indicates that the famine in Canaan was severe. The Hebrew word translated "severe" means "burdensome" or "difficult." Remember that when Abram first heard the call of God, he was in his birthplace, Ur of the Chaldeans—a port city of luxurious comfort, fed by two great rivers, resulting in rich soil and plentiful harvests. Canaan, on the other hand, had an exceedingly fragile ecology, making it subject to famine at any time. If rains did not come at the needed time, or if it rained too much or too little, planting and harvesting were adversely affected.[39]

Can you imagine what Abram thought as he realized the land the Lord promised him would not be able to feed his family? He probably started questioning the will of God for his life. How many times have you stepped out in faith, and when you arrived and were faced with difficulty thought, "I made a mistake."

That's our tendency as humans. Often the challenge we face when hurdles come our way is that we doubt the will of God. Somehow we get the notion that being in the center of God's will means everything will run smoothly. Quite the contrary! God will often send us through demanding circumstances to mature us. We must meet the challenge, trust the will of God, and recognize that trials come from the hand of a sovereign Lord.

It's not surprising that Abram doubted God when we remember the promises the Lord gave to him in Genesis 12:2–3. God told Abram that he would take care of him and bless him as he set out on his journey, yet here was Abram faced with hunger and fear—a fear that undermined his ability to trust God.

---

[39]Walter and Matthews 36–37.

We live in a sinful environment that is spiritually, physically, emotionally, and mentally challenging to the life of faith. Because sin consumes our environment, we may be faced daily with circumstances that will test and try our faith. If we respond with a wholehearted trust in God, our faith will not falter, but if fear overcomes faith, faith will falter.[40]

Abram did not pass God's test of faith. His lack of trust caused him to take matters into his own hands. Fear overcame faith, and Abram faltered as he used his wife and lied to attempt to override the sovereignty of God. How can we keep our faith from faltering? We must realize that fear is the greatest enemy to the life of faith.

The Greatest Enemy to the Life of Faith is Fear (12:10–16)

Franklin Roosevelt once said, "The only thing we have to fear is fear itself." In our spiritual life, fear is our greatest enemy. Now, fear can be a friend to faith if we let it strengthen our faith (for example, if we exhibit a reverential fear of God), but more often than not our fear will overcome faith. Genesis 12:10–16 illustrates how Abram gave into fear and how our fright can speak louder than the Father.

Fear Can Speak Louder than the Father

In verse 10 we are told that because of the famine in the land, Abram decided to leave the place where God commanded him to go and make his way into Egypt. At first glance this seems like the wise thing to do, but when you take a closer look at the verse you notice that something is missing.

---

[40]Gene A. Getz, *Abraham: Holding Fast the Will of God* (Nashville: Broadman and Holman, 1996) 41.

We know from the previous passages that the Lord brought Abram out of Ur of the Chaldeans with his father Terah. We know from Genesis 12:1 that it was the Lord who commanded Abram to leave Haran and go to Canaan. What is missing in this journey? The voice of the Lord telling Abram to go to Egypt. The absence of God speaking to Abram is no coincidence; it reveals that Abram was letting his fear speak louder than the Father.

Abram now placed God's promises in the background and let his fears speak to him. He probably thought, "Will God really take care of me? Is he really going to bless me as he promised?" These doubts started to chip away at Abram's trust in the Lord and began to overshadow his knowledge of God's promises. Abram's view of reality became distorted, and he lost sight of God.

Let's not be too hard on Abram. He's certainly not alone. In Numbers 13 and 14, God's people let their fears speak louder than the promises of the Father when God commanded Moses to take leaders from the twelve tribes of Israel and send them into the land of Canaan. Twelve men spent forty days spying out the land. When they returned, they declared that the land had much to offer, but ten of them were terrified to go in. They saw that the people were gigantic and incredibly strong; therefore, they thought the Israelites should not go in. However, two of the twelve men, Caleb and Joshua, disagreed. Needless to say, the ten whose fear overtook them influenced the rest of the sons of Israel, and the people cried and rebelled against the Lord. They forgot the Lord's promise to give them the land. They forgot God's promise to take care of them. Their fears spoke louder than the Father's promises.

Much like the Israelites, Abram fell into this pattern of fear and, if we are not careful, so will we. We will take things into our own hands instead of trusting the Lord.

Fear Causes Us to Take Things into Our Own Hands

Notice that in verse 1, God took the initiative to summons Abram to the journey of faith. However, beginning in verse 10, Abram took the lead. He determined on his own to "[go] down to Egypt." The reason is simple: his faith had faltered on account of his fears. Abram took things into his own hands and left God out of the equation.[41]

Abram's sojourn into Egypt was a clear indication that he was operating on his own terms and not on the Father's. There are a few times in the Bible where we see the Lord commanding or allowing his people to go to Egypt. A later account in Genesis informs us that "God told Jacob to go to Egypt" (Genesis 46:3). In the New Testament, an angel of the Lord told Joseph to take Mary and baby Jesus to Egypt to keep the baby from harm (Matthew 2:13). But for the most part, when Egypt is mentioned in the Bible, it usually refers to that which is of the world. To go to and to rely on Egypt is symbolic of relying on human resources rather than trusting in the Lord.[42] Typically, when God's people find themselves in Egypt, it is because their faith has faltered, they have taken things into their own hands, and they are trusting in human instead of divine resources, which usually results in a downward effect. That is, the lack of faith often leads to more sin. And that is exactly what happened to Abram; he continued on this downhill spiral of sin. When faith falters it can cause God's people to do things in the flesh.

Fear Causes Us to Do Things in the Flesh

When you see the actions of Abram in verses 11 through 13 you begin to think that Abram never responded to God's summons to the life of faith. Abram's actions in this passage were no different

---

[41]Kidner 116.
[42]Boice 472.

than an unbeliever's actions. Abram acted totally apart from God. Like an unbeliever who has no faith, Abram feared famine and doubted God's ability to provide him with daily sustenance, and he feared the Egyptians and doubted God's ability to protect him from danger. Therefore, Abram resorted to scheming and deception for the purpose of protecting his own life. Notice the conversation that took place between Abram and Sarai just before they entered Egypt. "And it came about when he came near to Egypt, that he said to Sarai his wife, "See now, I know that you are a beautiful woman; and it will come about when the Egyptians see you, that they will say 'This is his wife'; and they will kill me, but they will let you live. Please say that you are my sister so that it may go well with me because of you, and that I may live on account of you" (Genesis 12:11–13).

Abram knew that the Egyptians would kill him on account of Sarai. If he told the Egyptians he was Sarai's brother, it would buy them time to escape because the Egyptians would negotiate with Abram for the right to marry his sister. But if they knew Abram was Sarai's husband, then they would just kill him.[43]

Therefore, Abram took things into his own hands. There is some truth that Abram is Sarai's brother. Genesis 20:12 says that Sarai is Abram's half sister, but why would Abram resort to deception and half-truths? Because at this point it was all about him. He didn't want to die, so he did things in the flesh. He made a plan to protect himself and to "help" the Lord keep his promise.

A former classmate of mine had a pastorate in a small town just north of Denton, Texas. One Monday evening he called me to tell me how bad his day went. He had spent the morning at the hospital because one of his deacons had passed away. When he arrived back at the church and the parsonage, he found the fire department there putting out a massive grass fire that had consumed the cemetery and about thirteen acres of a church member's property behind the church. What made this situation

---

[43]Ross 275.

even worse is that my friend knew that the bonfire he and his youth minister started behind the church the night before caused the destructive fire. Then the church member who owned the land behind the church asked my friend if he knew how the fire started. In fear, my friend lied and told him that he didn't. Of course the Holy Spirit did not let him get away with the lie, and he had to tell the member the truth. My friend, as many of us have done, let his fear overcome his faith for self-preservation.

In the same manner, Abram's fear caused him to act in the flesh and devise his own plan for preservation, but as we'll soon see, Abram's fleshly and ungodly plan would backfire on him. "It came about when Abram came into Egypt, the Egyptians saw the woman was very beautiful. Pharaoh's officials saw her and praised her to Pharaoh; and the woman was taken into Pharaoh's house. Therefore he treated Abram well for her sake; and gave him sheep and oxen and donkeys and male and female servants and female donkeys and camels" (Genesis 12:14–16).

Abram was correct in saying they would see that Sarai was very beautiful. Abram was also correct that if they thought he was Sarai's brother, it would go well with him and his life would be spared. But Abram was wrong about having enough time to negotiate with the Egyptians. His false calculation would put his wife and his marriage in danger.

Though Abram experienced the blessings bestowed upon him from Pharaoh, these blessings were not divine; instead, they came through human initiative. Just because a believer is being blessed materially does not indicate divine favor. Abram prospered materially, but he was spiritually rundown. Furthermore, God's promise to make Abram a great nation and bless all nations through him was based upon the seed of Abram, a promise that was now in jeopardy because of Abram's faltering faith.

You could say that Abram left one problem only to find himself with another. He left a physical famine only to found himself with a spiritual hunger, one that came upon him on the basis of his faltering faith in the Lord's ability to take care of him. When our faith falters and we take things into our own hands, we can be assured that our problems will not be solved. We merely exchange one challenging circumstance for another.

The greatest enemy to the life of faith is unhealthy fear. Fear can either draw us close to God or drive us far from him. The latter is the greatest enemy of God. When fear begins to drive us away from God it does so by speaking louder than the promises of God. When fear speaks louder than the Father, we are often tempted to take things in our own hands, that is, to do things "in the flesh" rather than to rely on God. But all is not lost when our faith falters, for when our faith falters we can be assured that our faithful God will not.

When Our Faith Falters, Our Faithful God Will Not (12:17–13:4)

In verse 17 we see the faithful Lord intervene, "But the Lord …" Those three words are a declaration of God's faithfulness. In fact, this story of Abram's faltering faith is more about a faithful God than it is about a faithless servant. Though Abram's faltering faith would jeopardize the promise of God, God's faithfulness to his word would bring the promise about. In making sure that his promise would be fulfilled, we see God's faithfulness revealed in three different ways. The first thing we see is God's faithfulness to intervene and discipline the faltering faith.

Faithful to Discipline

> But the Lord struck Pharaoh and his house with great plagues because of Sarai, Abram's wife. Then Pharaoh called Abram and said, "What is this you have done to me? Why did you not tell me that she was your wife? Why did you say, 'She

> is my sister,' so that I took her for my wife?' "
> (Genesis 12:17–19)

If we are tempted to think that the Lord approves of Abram's behavior, then verses 17 through 19 should dispel any such notions. Abram left one challenging circumstance and found himself in another. It would seem that trouble was on the horizon. Abram was helpless to save his wife Sarai, but God was not.[44] God would intervene by first bringing discipline upon Pharaoh and then by using Pharaoh to discipline Abram's faltering faith.

Verse 17 declares that the Lord struck Pharaoh and his house with a plague or disease. Without any question, Pharaoh understood that the disease was the consequence of taking Sarai into his household. In the ancient world the assumption was that when disease or sickness occurred it was always a direct result of a god's displeasure. The pagan religions saw disease and sickness as a direct result of sin.[45] The Lord revealed to Pharaoh that Sarai was Abram's wife, and as a result the Lord struck Pharaoh and his household with disease.

Pharaoh then called Abram to him and rebuked him for his faltering faith. But don't think for a minute that the source of the rebuke is Pharaoh. The Lord used a pagan ruler to rebuke his servant. Twice Pharaoh asked Abram why he lied to him. This rebuke is indicative of just how far out of fellowship Abram was with the Lord. Before Abram left for Egypt the Lord spoke to him personally, appeared to him, and Abram worshipped and called upon the name of the Lord. But in Egypt the Lord was silent, Abram's worship was absent, and the Lord used an ungodly man to rebuke a man of God.

Listen to Pharaoh's questions once again, but this time hear them as coming from the very mouth of the Lord, "Why did you not tell me she was your wife? Why did you say, 'She is my sister,' so that I took her for my wife?" The Lord confronted

---

[44]Henry M. Morris, *The Genesis Record* (Grand Rapids: Baker, 1976) 300.
[45]Walton and Matthews 38.

Abram on his faltering faith, and if Abram were honest with God he would have to say that he lied because his faith faltered back in Canaan. He lied because he failed to trust God in the Promised Land, and he took things into his own hands to try to take care of himself. Really all Abram had to do was to trust the Lord.

The Lord's rebuke through Pharaoh demonstrates God's faithfulness to discipline his straying children. God intervened in the life of Abram because his word and his character were at stake. The Lord deals with all of his children the same way he dealt with Abram. He is faithful to discipline and to deliver when his people's faith falters.

Faithful to Deliver

Verse 20 shows us that not only is the Lord faithful to discipline, but he is also faithful to deliver, "Pharaoh commanded his men concerning him; and they escorted him away, with his wife and all that belonged to him." Amazingly, Abram put himself and his wife in a predicament, one that could harm both of them, yet the Lord faithfully delivered them both unharmed. But we must be very careful to understand God's deliverance.

In this case, God delivered Abram from the consequences of his faltering faith, but God does not always do that. We can be assured that the Lord will deliver us spiritually by providing forgiveness and cleansing of our sins, but God often does not deliver us from the consequences of our sins.[46] We see that take place time and again with the people of Israel. We especially see that take place in the life of King David. David committed adultery and murder, the Lord forgave him, but he did not deliver him from the consequences of his sin.

Some time ago a story came out about a pharmacist who was watering down chemo treatments to make money. It turned out that this pharmacist was a Christian man who was trying to

---

[46]Ross 277.

pay off taxes and a financial commitment he made to his church. This Christian brother confessed his faltering faith and the Lord has forgiven him, but the Lord did not deliver him from the consequences of his sin—he served time in prison.

Faithful to Direct

The first four verses of Genesis 13 reveals a final observation about God's faithfulness when Abram's faith faltered. "So Abram went up from Egypt to the Negev, he and his wife and all that belonged to him, and Lot with him. Now Abram was very rich in livestock, in silver and gold. He went on his journeys from the Negev as far as Bethel, to the place where his tent had been at the beginning, between Bethel and Ai, to the place of the altar which he had made there formerly; and there Abram called on the name of the Lord."

In these passages, God in his faithfulness, directed Abram when his faith faltered. Abram went as far as Bethel, which means "house of God." He went back to where he started, that is, back to where he was before his faith faltered. Compare this to verse 8 of chapter 12, "Then he proceeded from there to the mountain on the east of Bethel, and pitched his tent, with Bethel on the west and Ai on the east; and there he built an alter to the Lord and called upon the name of the Lord." God was faithful to forgive Abram's faltering faith and direct him into full fellowship once again.

Abram came full circle. His faltering faith led him away from the Lord, away from worshipping him, away from calling upon him and listening to him, but the Lord led Abram back to the place he never should have left, the presence of the Lord.

A pastor visited one of his church members who happened to be a farmer. When he got out of his car he noticed an inscription on the farmer's windmill: "God is faithful." The pastor asked the farmer, "Is that to mean that depending on what direction the wind is blowing God is faithful?" The farmer said, "Absolutely not! I put that there to remind me that no matter what direction the wind blows or whether the wind blows, God is always faithful."

The lesson for keeping our faith from faltering should not be centered on the faithlessness of Abram. If we are truly going to keep our faith from faltering, then we need to focus on the faithfulness of God that is revealed in this passage. When fear comes our way, we don't need more faith. Instead we need a greater understanding of the object of our faith. We must remember that the Lord is always faithful, in feast or in famine, whether the wind blows or not. Because our God is absolutely faithful, when challenging circumstances come our way, when fear is creeping at our door, we can be assured that the Lord will take care of us.

CHAPTER III:

HOW THE LIFE OF FAITH DEALS WITH CONFLICT

Genesis 13:1–18

Introduction

Through experience I have learned that a great deal of conflict that occurs within the family of faith is often among church staff members. There's the story about the friction between one pastor and his music director—conflict that was so great it spilled out into the worship service.

One Sunday the pastor preached on total commitment to the Lord, and the music minister followed with the congregation singing "I Shall Not Be Moved." The next Sunday the pastor preached on giving and how God's people should give generously to the Lord. The disgruntled music director led the congregation in "Jesus Paid it All." The following Sunday the pastor preached on gossip and the need to control the tongue, and the music leader followed with "I Love to Tell the Story."

At this point the pastor was frustrated and he told the church that he was considering resigning on the next Sunday. The music leader then led the song "Oh, Why Not Tonight." The following Sunday the pastor stood in the pulpit and said, "Jesus led me to this church and it is Jesus who is leading me away." The song leader's selection that day was "What a Friend We Have in Jesus."

Our study of the life of Abram will teach God's people how to deal with conflict when it comes our way. The lessons we will learn in this chapter of Abram's journey of faith are in stark contrast to those we learned in the previous chapter when Abram failed to trust the Lord. Now we are going to learn from Abram's ability to trust in the Lord in the midst of friction and conflict. Why such a stark contrast between the two narratives? What was the source of Abram's previous failure and his upcoming success?

Both Abram's success and his failure in the life of faith hinged on one crucial ingredient: fellowship with the Lord. As we noticed in the verses we've studied so far, the key ingredient missing in Abram's failure was the altar of the Lord. Worship, fellowship, and communication with the Lord were non-existent in Genesis 12:10–20. But not so in Genesis 13.

The Lord, faithful to discipline Abram's faltering faith and deliver him from the situation, was also faithful to direct him back to where he needed to be. "He went on his journeys from the Negev as far as Bethel, to the place where his tent had been at the beginning, between Bethel and Ai, to the place of the altar which he had made there formerly; and there Abram called upon the name of the Lord" (Genesis 13:3–4).

God brought Abram back to where he needed to be in the first place: the altar of the Lord. If Abram were going to have success and keep his faith from faltering, he would need to maintain constant worship of and fellowship and communication with the Lord. Let's see it in practice now.

Genesis 13 begins with Abram at the altar and ends with him at the altar. "He went on his journeys from the Negev as far as Bethel, to the place where his tent had been at the beginning, between Bethel and Ai, to *the place of the altar* which he had made there formerly; and there Abram called on the name of the LORD" (Genesis 13:3–4, emphasis added). Also, "Then Abram moved his tent and came and dwelt by the oaks of Mamre, which are in Hebron, and there *he built an altar to the Lord*" (Genesis 13:18, emphasis added). The key to success in the life of faith is constant communion with the Lord. This steadfast fellowship with the Lord will give Abram success as he faces friction within the family. His success in dealing with this strife can teach us how to deal with conflict. But before we learn how to deal with conflict, we must come to grips with the fact that conflict is inevitable, even within the family of faith.

Conflict Will Be Experienced within the Family of Faith

The following verses set the scene, as we understand the nature of the conflict that is experienced between uncle and nephew. Verses 5 and 6 reveal the source of the conflict.

> Now Lot, who went with Abram, also had flocks and herds and tents. And the land could not sustain them while dwelling together, for their possessions were so great that they were not able to remain together. And there was strife between the herdsmen of Abram's livestock and the herdsman of Lot's livestock. Now the Canaanite and the Perizzite were dwelling then in the Land. (Genesis 13:5–7)

The Source of the Conflict

We are told in verse 5 that Lot was with Abram when he went into Egypt. Some have argued that the phrase, "who went with Abram" is artificial and was placed there only to make it appear that Lot was in Egypt. They argue this on the basis that Lot is not mentioned in verses 10 through 20. However, the absence of Lot in the previous narrative was because he was not a central figure of the situation. The main characters in those verses were Abram, Sarai, and Pharaoh.

While Lot was in Egypt with his uncle, he was able to observe first hand his uncle's faltering faith. He saw his uncle put his own interest before his wife's. Lot watched as his uncle took things into his own hands, walking by sight rather than by faith. What Lot witnessed of his uncle's faltering faith would have an effect on the choices he would make.

Our text not only implicitly declares that Lot was able to witness Abram's faltering faith, but it also explicitly states that the blessings given to Abram were conferred upon Lot as well. Verse 5 reveals that Lot also had "flocks and herds and tents." Lot profited by the illegitimate blessings gained by his uncle.

The blessings Abram and Lot enjoyed came about by Abram not trusting in God, taking things into his own hands, and lying and scheming to save his own life, while forgetting about the danger that he put his wife in, and even the danger he put his nephew in. These illegitimate blessings that Abram and Lot received would become a source of conflict within the family.

The reason for contention within the family is revealed in verse 6, "And the land could not sustain them while dwelling together, for their possessions were so great that they were not able to remain together." Abram and Lot were so prosperous that the land of promise given by the Lord would not supply all they needed. For all their livestock, Abram and Lot had an inadequate supply of pasturage and water.[47] Because Abram and Lot were not the only ones dwelling in the land (they shared the land with the Canaanites and Perizzites, v. 7), the availability of pastureland and water was limited. The result of limited natural resources caused problems, "And there was strife between the herdsmen of Abram and the herdsmen of Lot" (v. 7). Prosperity did not bring comfort to the family, instead it brought conflict, which began between Abram and Lot's herdsmen.

---

[47]Walton and Matthews 38.

There is something very interesting in these verses that I want to point out. It was back in Genesis 12:10 that Abram, who was exactly where God wanted him to be, experienced famine in the land. Back in Genesis 12:16 Abram was in Egypt where God did not want him, yet everything went well for him there. And here in verses 5 and 6 of Genesis 13, Abram is exactly where God wants him, but now he is facing conflict within the family. Even when we do exactly what God wants, he allows trials. This passage of Scripture shows the Lord sending another challenging circumstance Abram's way to test his faith. This time, Abram will pass the test.[48]

Just as conflict was experienced in the family of Abram, we will also experience contention in the church. The sources of conflict are many, but the need to deal with them in a way consistent with the life of faith is paramount. The family of faith suffers serious implications when we do not deal with conflict in a biblical manner.

The Seriousness of the Conflict

The seriousness of conflict is implied in verse 7, "Now the Canaanite and the Perizzite were dwelling then in the land." This verse not only declares the reason for the land's inability to sustain Abram and Lot's livestock, but it also reveals the dangers that take place when there is strife within the family. The first serious consequence of conflict is that the family of faith will become ineffective and vulnerable.[49]

When the Lord called Abram to leave his country, he called him to leave a peaceful country and go to a land that would be filled with hostility. There would be people in the land who would be enemies of Abram and his descendants; the Canaanites and the Perizzites were those enemies.

---

[48]Steward Briscoe, *Mastering the Old Testament: Genesis* (Dallas: Word Publishing, 1987) 132.
[49]*The NET Bible* 54.

Internal conflict among Abram's relatives would weaken the family and leave them ineffective and vulnerable in fighting the true enemy at hand. The battle that God's people are to be fighting is not on the inside, but on the outside. When conflict abounds within the family of faith it weakens the family's effectiveness in fulfilling God's purpose and plan, which is to bless all the families of the earth with the good news of salvation found in Christ.

A father asked his young son to break a bundle of sticks. The boy raised the bundle off the ground and smashed it with his knee leaving the bundle unbroken and his knee bruised. He then took the bundle and set it against the wall and stomped on it with his foot, but the bundle still did not break. He came back to his father frustrated from the chore that his father had given him. The father, seeing the boy's frustration, took the bundle of sticks and untied it. He then took the sticks and broke them easily, one at a time. When the family of faith is united they are strong and effective, but a divided family of faith is weak and ineffective for the work of the Lord.[50]

Another serious implication of conflict is that it makes the family of faith repulsive. Abram was to be a blessing bearer to the world. He was to carry the light of the one true God to the pagan nations. Conflict within his family could hinder the testimony of God's people. Conflict over material possessions was a poor testimony to the ungodly Canaanites in the land. Likewise, when conflict abounds in the church, it gives an appalling testimony to the ungodly outside the church.[51] Nobody in his or her right mind would want to be a part of such a situation.

The world is looking for a safe haven, a place where peace and love abounds, and that place must be the family of faith, that place must be the church of Jesus Christ. People should

---

[50]Michael P. Green, *1500 Illustrations for Biblical Preaching* (Grand Rapids: Baker, 1989) 66.

[51]John Phillips, *Exploring Genesis* (Grand Rapids: Kregel, 1980) 122.

come and experience the love and acceptance of Christ when they come to the family of faith, not the constant bickering and conflict. And while conflict is inevitably experienced within the church family, believers must resolve the conflict in a manner consistent with the life of faith.

Resolve Conflict in a Manner Consistent with a Life of Faith

Abram's conflict would put his faith to the test once again, but this time his faith would flourish, not falter. Abram would trust the Lord to take care of him in the midst of this test, rather than to take things into his own hands. His response to the conflict is consistent with those who trust in the Lord to take care of them. The first quality we see in the life of Abram that is consistent with the life of faith is the desire of a peaceful resolution.

The Life of Faith Desires a Peaceful Resolution

> So Abram said to Lot, "Please let there be no strife between you and me, nor between my herdsmen and your herdsmen, for we are brothers." (Genesis 13:8)

Abram's desire in the midst of this conflict is a peaceful resolution. Though the previous verse (v. 7) spoke of the strife only being between the herdsmen, Abram understood that this conflict would spill over into the family. Therefore, Abram pleaded with Lot for a peaceful solution, knowing there could be serious repercussions if the conflict was not dealt with properly. He knew that it could weaken the family, make them vulnerable to their real enemies, and that the testimony of the Lord could be hindered. These are great reasons for dealing with conflict, but Abram gave the paramount reason at the end of verse 8.

The most significant reason that Abram sought a peaceful settlement is stated in the prepositional phrase "for we are brothers." Abram did not say that he and Lot were brothers in the literal sense, for we know that Abram was Lot's uncle. Abram used the word "brother" to declare their close relationship to one another. That Abram and Lot were family was reason to seek a peaceful resolution. Yes, it is valuable to pursue peace for the sake effectiveness, and it is worthy to seek peace for the sake of testimony, but more importantly, it is necessary to seek a peace to maintain the family bond.

We who are a part of the family of God are brothers and sisters in Christ. We are in a relationship with one another that will last throughout eternity. Therefore, since we are bound together by the blood of Christ, we must seek a peaceful outcome when conflict arises. Jesus said, "Blessed are the peacemakers, for they shall be called sons of God" (Matthew 5:9).

One story has it that during the Civil War, the North and the South were camped on opposite sides of the Potomac River. The Union soldiers would play a patriotic tune that was dear to their hearts. In response, the Confederate soldiers would play a patriotic tune precious to southerners. Then one of the bands started to play the tune "Home, Sweet, Home." The other side stopped its musical composition and joined in. Soon after that you could hear voices from both sides singing, "There is no place like home."[52]

Though division existed between the Union and Confederate soldiers, the song reminded them that their home and their destiny were the same. Likewise, members of God's family must remember that as brothers and sister we have the same eternal home; therefore, we must desire a peaceful resolution when conflict arises.

---

[52]Green 68.

The Life of Faith Initiates a Peaceful Resolution

Abram not only desired a peaceful resolution to the situation, but he also took the initiative to bring it about. How did Abram take the initiative? He put his total trust in the Lord to take care of his needs as implied in Genesis 13:9, "Is not the whole land before you? Please separate from me; if to the left, then I will go to the right, or if to the right, then I will go to the left."

Abram could have demanded his rights regarding who goes where. After all, he was the uncle, the elder, and God had given him the land. Abram could have told Lot exactly what to do, but he didn't. This time, Abram put God first in his life. He had learned a great lesson in Egypt: trust the Lord in all situations. Because Abram put God first and trusted in the Lord to take care of him, he was able to put others second and still take care of their needs.[53]

William Booth, the founder of the Salvation Army, became very sick in his latter years—so sick that he was unable to attend the annual Salvation Army conferences. Each year Booth would send a message to be read to the delegates. One time he sent a simple message that read, "Others." The philosophy of the Salvation Army was to look out for the interest of others.[54] All Christians need the same attitude. Paul told the Philippians to "not merely look out for [their] own personal interests, but also for the interests of others" (Philippians 2:4).

When God's people put God first and trust him to take care of their needs, it is revealed in selfless living. The Lord Jesus Christ is the greatest example of one who demonstrated total trust in the Lord and unselfish living. He was entitled to demand his rights, but instead he suffered at the hands of sinful men for the sake of others. He emptied himself of his glory, became a servant, and was obedient unto death. Christ trusted in the Father

---

[53]Warren W. Wiersbe, *Be Obedient* (Colorado Springs: Chariot Victor Publishers, 1991), 28.
[54]Wiersbe 28.

to take care of him, he put others first, and the Father exalted him. And now every knee should bow and every tongue confess that Jesus Christ is Lord (Philippians 2:5–11).

Abram's total reliance on the Lord and his self-sacrificing living is contrasted with Lot's distrust in the Lord and his selfish ways. Lot's choice in verses 10–11 resemble the choice that his uncle made when he went into Egypt. Like his uncle, Lot would choose based on sight instead of faith.

When Abram gave Lot the choice, the proper godly response would be to defer to his elder uncle. "Lot lifted up his eyes and saw all the valley of the Jordan." Instead of deferring to the true warranted rights of his uncle, Lot looked out only for himself instead of putting God first and others second.

What did Lot see when he lifted up his eyes and gazed upon the valley of the Jordan? The text says that Lot saw that "it was well watered everywhere—this was before the Lord destroyed Sodom and Gomorrah—like the garden of the Lord, like the land of Egypt as you go to Zoar" (v. 10). At a glance, what Lot saw looked profitable and appealing, but we'll soon see that it would not be beneficial at all.

Verse 10 forewarns the readers that Lot's self-gratifying and self-seeking response would bring blessings, but those blessings would be temporal.[55] Nestled within the description of what Lot saw is the statement, "this was before the Lord destroyed Sodom and Gomorrah." Lot was seeking to take care of himself without the Lord's help, and his self-centered choice would bring disaster. "So Lot chose for himself all the valley of the Jordan, and Lot journeyed eastward" (v. 11). Lot's choice was all about himself; he exhibited no concern for his uncle. One scholar commented, "Lot selfishly intends to advantage himself by disadvantaging his uncle."[56]

It is significant to notice that when Lot made his choice he "journeyed eastward." Since the banishment of Adam and Eve

---

[55]Ross 289.
[56]Waltke 222.

from the Garden of Eden the "east" came to symbolize distance and exile from the presence of God. Lot would soon find out that being distanced from the divine presence would not lead to divine blessing.

Fortunately, Abram's response to the conflict did not mirror Lot's response. For had Abram responded in selfishness as Lot did, the conflict would not have be dealt with in a peaceful manner, and the effectiveness and the testimony of God's people would have been hindered. Because Abram dealt with the conflict in a manner consistent with the life of faith, he gained a peaceful resolution.

The Life of Faith Gains a Peaceful Resolution

So, Abram and Lot went their separate ways in peace. "So Lot chose for himself all the valley of the Jordan, and Lot journeyed eastward. Thus they separated from each other. Abram settled in the land of Canaan, while Lot settled in the cities of the valley and moved his tents as far as Sodom. Now the men of Sodom were wicked exceedingly and sinners against the Lord" (Genesis 13:11–13).

Can you imagine what the outcome would have been if Abram responded to the conflict in the same manner that Lot did? It would have been disastrous. Had Abram responded with selfish motives, with self-gratification in mind, there might have been a civil war. But Abram trusted the Lord to look out for him, enabling him to look out for Lot and stay at peace.

How did they gain a peaceful resolution? Through separation. There are times when, for the sake of peace, the family of faith needs to separate. If there are disagreements about methods, then separate peacefully and reach people for the cause of Christ. Separation should take place to prevent the church from feuding and warring against one another. Unfortunately, it has been my experience that separation takes place only after feuding and fighting has permeated the family of faith. (Note that

I do not use the term "separate" to condone separation between husband and wife—the context here is about unmarried believers within the body of Christ who are not married to each other and who are at odds.)

Abram saw the potential of prolonged conflict; therefore, he took the initiative to bring about a peaceful resolution, and he gained it because he dealt with the conflict in a manner worthy of a life of faith. Abram's trust in the Lord during conflict would not go unnoticed. For the Lord would affirm his approval of Abram's faith and trust by showering divine confirmation. "The LORD said to Abram, after Lot had separated from him, 'Now lift up your eyes and look from the place where you are, northward and southward and eastward and westward; for all the land which you see, I will give it to you and to your descendants forever. I will make your descendants as the dust of the earth, so that if anyone can number the dust of the earth, then your descendants can also be numbered' " (Genesis 13:14–18).

The Confirmation upon the Life of Faith (14–16)

Genesis 13:14–18 is set apart by the words, "The Lord said to Abram." These are words of comfort as well as cause. They are comforting because God is reaffirming his promise to Abram and he is telling us that when we trust in him, even in the midst of conflict, he will take care of his own.

These words of the Lord were also the cause of Abram's faith. Abram took the Lord at his word; therefore, Abram could give Lot first choice because he had learned what the Lord has said to him when he called him to the life of faith—that God would take care of his needs. Abram could look out for the interests of others because he knew that the Lord would be faithful to fulfill his promises, even when Abram was unfaithful.[57] At this point Abram knew that God meant what he

---

[57]Ross 288.

had said, and that it did not matter what choice Lot made because God had enough room in his plan for every man, and God would take care of Abram.[58]

In these verses the Lord reaffirmed his promises to Abram, which he initially gave in Genesis 12:2–3. In reaffirming his promises, notice the stark contrast between Abram and the narrative of Lot in the previous verses.

The Lord said to Abram, "Lift up your eyes and look from the place where you are, northward and southward and eastward and westward; for all the land that you see, I will give it to you and to your descendants forever." Here, the Lord commanded Abram to lift up his eyes, whereas in the previous verses Lot lifted up his eyes. In this passage, the Lord told Abram to look, whereas in the preceding passage, Lot was the one who saw. Now we read that the Lord gave all the land to Abram, whereas before, Lot chose all the land of the valley. Abram waited for God to take the initiative, Lot simply took his own initiative. Abram waited for God to give him the land, Lot simply took for himself.[59]

It is hard to believe that this is the same Abram who went into Egypt. It is safe to say that this stage of Abram's journey of faith was successful. It was a period when Abram was tested by inward strife, but instead of his faith faltering it flourished, and the Lord took care of him.

The Communion of the Life of Faith (17–18)

The key to Abram's flourishing faith is found once again in his communion with the Lord. When Abram walked with and worshipped the Lord, his faith was strong. But when he turned from the Lord and forsook sweet fellowship with the Lord, his

---

[58]Ross 288.
[59]Ross 288.

faith faltered. Observe Abram's acts of communion and worship in verses 17 and 18 after God spoke to Abram.

" 'Arise, walk about the land through its length and breadth; for I will give it to you.' Then Abram moved his tent and came and dwelt by the oaks of Mamre, which are in Hebron, and there he built an altar to the Lord."

In verse 17 the Lord commanded Abram to "arise" and "walk about." God's purpose in this command was to remind Abram that he would give Abram and his descendants the land. We also see Abram maintain communion with God through his worship. Verse 18 declares that Abram built an altar to the Lord, a sign of Abram's devotion and gratitude toward the Lord. It was Abram's maintained daily communion with the Lord that enabled him to respond to the conflict in a manner consistent with the life of faith. Abram's daily walk with and worship of the Lord made it possible for him to respond correctly to the conflict with Lot and allowed him to put God first, then others, and finally himself.

A 1970s poet once wrote, "All I ask of life is a constant and exaggerated sense of my own importance." Obviously ego was in charge of this person's life. But for one who lives in daily communion with the Lord, our motto should be, "All I ask of life is a constant and exaggerated sense of the importance of trusting the Lord and putting others before myself." Only one who fully trusts in the Lord can claim this motto.

A father was in his study reading when he overheard his daughter and her friend outside. What began as harmless play suddenly sound like an argument. The conversation between the two girls became heated and argumentative. The father decided it was time to step in, so he opened the window and said, "Stop it. Honey, what's wrong?" His daughter quickly responded, "But, Daddy, we were just playing church."[60]

There is no doubt that the family of faith will experience conflict. It takes humility to deal with conflict in a manner

---

[60]Charles R. Swindoll, *The Tale of the Tardy Oxcart* (Nashville: Word Publishing, 1998) 95.

consistent with the life of faith. We can cultivate humility only if we individually foster our daily walk with the Lord and reverently worship him. We can also put others before ourselves knowing that the Lord will take care of our every need.

Chapter IV:

Spiritual People Involved in Spiritual Warfare

Genesis 14:1–24

John Milton, in his great works *Paradise Lost* and *Paradise Regained*, spoke about the great cosmic combat that occurs in Revelation 12. In describing that chilling chapter of Revelation, Milton says that heaven and hell are the central focus, and earth is the battleground in which the cosmic combat takes place.[61] That is an accurate description of the spiritual battle that happens within our world.

With all the talk about war going on in our own society and around the world, Christians often forget that we are in a war of our own, a spiritual war, a cosmic combat. The battle is between heaven and hell, but the fight is here on earth.

The church often loses sight of the truth of spiritual struggle. American Christians have become so comfortable in our Christianity that the thought of spiritual warfare hardly even crosses our minds. But it is paramount that we understand that the

---

[61]Philip Yancy, "CT Classic: Cosmic Combat Part 3," *Christianity Today Magazine* 1 December 1999 <http://www.christianitytoday.com/ct/1999/decemberweb-only/46.0b.html>.

Lord has called his people to fight a spiritual battle, to wage war against the forces that oppose God's righteousness and rule.

Understanding the nature of spiritual warfare begins with understanding the nature of the life of faith. You could say that the life of faith is really a "life of war." Yet, the war that we fight is not fought with conventional weapons nor is it fought against flesh and blood. Instead, we fight spiritual wars with spiritual weapons against spiritual enemies.

There is no greater description of this type of spiritual warfare in the New Testament than that found in the book of Ephesians where Paul gave Christians a command to "be strong in the Lord and in the strength of his might" (Eph. 6:10). To be "in the Lord" is to be a spiritual person, one who has started the life of faith by following Jesus Christ. Thus, it takes spiritual people to handle spiritual combat.

Furthermore it takes spiritual weapons to fight a spiritual enemy. Paul describes these weapons as the armor of God, which consists of truth, righteousness, the gospel, faith, salvation, the Holy Spirit, the word of God, and prayer. We need spiritual weapons because "our struggle is not against flesh and blood, but against the rulers, against the powers, against the world forces of this darkness, against the *spiritual* forces of wickedness in the heavenly places" (Eph. 6:12, emphasis added).

Our study of the life of Abraham supports that what is true of those who live the life of faith under the New Covenant was also true of believers under the Old Covenant. But notice in Genesis 14 that the spiritual battles Abram fought often worked themselves out in physical battles against the enemies of God and his people. This was also true of Moses and of Joshua. And because these physical battles were the manifestation of spiritual struggles, we as God's people can glean great truths for our own cosmic conflicts.

The life of faith is a life of war with spiritual bullets and missiles flying overhead. Those who are on the journey of faith cannot merely ignore the fight; they must be aware of it, but even more importantly, they must get involved.

The Involvement in Spiritual Warfare (v. 1–16)

In the first sixteen verses of Genesis 14, we see conflict, casualties, and contribution. The conflict is described in the first eleven verses of the chapter.

The Conflict

> And it came about in the days of Amraphel king of Shinar, Arioch king of Ellasar, Chedorlaomer king of Elam, and Tidal king of Goiim, that they made war with Bera king of Sodom, and with Birsha king of Gomorrah, Shinab king of Admah, and Shemeber king of Zeboiim, and the king of Bela (that is, Zoar). All these came as allies to the valley of Siddim (that is, the Salt Sea). Twelve years they had served Chedorlaomer, but the thirteenth year they rebelled. In the fourteenth year Chedorlaomer and the kings that were with him, came and defeated the Rephaim in Ashteroth-karnaim and the Zuzim in Ham and the Emim in Shaveh-kiriathaim, and the Horites in their Mount Seir, as far as El-paran, which is by the wilderness. Then they turned back and came to En-mishpat (that is, Kadesh), and conquered all the country of the Amalekites, and also the Amorites, who lived in Hazazon-tamar. And the king of Sodom and the king of Gomorrah and the king of Admah and the king of Zeboiim and the king of Bela (that is, Zoar) came out; and they arrayed for battle against them in the valley of Siddim, against Chedorlaomer king of Elam and Tidal king of Goiim and Amraphel king of Shinar and Arioch king of Ellasar—four kings against five. Now the valley of Siddim was full of tar pits;

> and the kings of Sodom and Gomorrah fled, and they fell into them. But those who survived fled to the hill country. Then they took all the goods of Sodom and Gomorrah and all their food supply, and departed. (Gen. 14:1–11)

The conflict recorded in these verses is on the international level—as "international" as Abram and his contemporaries knew, not on the international level we know. This is the first record of war and conflict in the Bible; some say it is the first record of war within the annals of history.[62]

The conflict takes place between nine kings, four on one side and five on the other. Because of the advantage of numbers, it would seem that the five kings would have more power, but as the record of the conflict unfolds, it is quite obvious that the smaller group of rulers was much more powerful.

Verse 1 introduces us to the four kings, "Amraphel the king of Shinar, Arioch king of Ellasar, Chedoorlaomer king of Elam, and Tidal king of Goiim." The four rulers were located east of the five kings, which today is in Iran and Turkey.[63] The five kings they warred against were the kings of Sodom, Gomorrah, Admah, Zeboiim, and Bela. They reigned in the same region Abram lived.

The reason for the war was not an uncommon one. Verse 4 gives an indication of why the war was taking place, "Twelve years they had served Chedorlaomer, but the thirteenth year they rebelled." The five kings served the four others for twelve years, but they finally had enough, so they rebelled. It was customary for the more powerful to ally together to subjugate those who were less powerful into serving them by paying tribute through means of money, produce, and other goods.[64] After twelve years

---

[62]Phillips 125.
[63]Walton and Matthews 39.
[64]Ross 298.

of paying tribute, the western kings decided that enough was enough.

It was highly probable that the five kings decided to rebel against the four because there were troubles in the eastern kingdoms that would keep them from taking action against the rebellion.[65] For though the rebellion took place in the thirteenth year, it wasn't until a year later that the four kings would respond (v. 5).

When the four kings finally did act against the rebellion, they began to make their way westward, a journey recorded in verses 6 through 8. Scholars believe they sojourned on what was known as the King's Highway. As the four kings made their way down the King's Highway to deal with the rebellion of the five kings, we are told in verses 5 and 6 that the four kings would defeat many others along the way. Most likely the rumors of their coming and their power was making its way to the five kings because we are told in verse 8 that the five kings came out to meet the four at the valley of Siddim.

It did not take long for the five kings to see their enemy's power, so they retreated. Some did not fair well in the retreat because they fell into the tar pits that made up that area. Those who did not fall into the tar pits retreated to the hills.

The retreat of the five kings left the town of those kings vulnerable. The four kings in verse 11 capitalized on this vulnerability. "Then they took all the goods of Sodom and Gomorrah and their food supply, and departed." If the five kings were not going to voluntarily pay tribute, then the four kings would take it by force.

Up to this point in the narrative it seems the story has nothing to do with Abram, but that changes in verse 12 when Abram would be brought into the battle, "They also took Lot, Abram's nephew, and his possessions and departed, for he was living in Sodom." Abram's nephew would become one of the casualties of the battle.

---

[65]Hartley 147.

The Casualties (12)

It is interesting to see the digression of Lot revealed in verse 12. According to Genesis 13:12, Lot moved his tents just outside of Sodom. But now Lot is no longer outside of Sodom; he is living in Sodom. In Genesis 13 we were warned about the poor choice Lot made to live in Sodom, and Genesis 14 reveals why it was a mistake.

But Lot is not the only casualty of the battle. One must understand that the four kings are being unjust. Subjugating weaker people for the purpose of personal gain is a grave injustice. Because the people who dwelt in the weaker cities were subjugated to the injustice, they also were casualties of the battle.

Furthermore, the scope of the spiritual war taking place surpasses any war that has ever taken place on earth. The spiritual war is a global war that is taking place in every country, city, church, home, and family. The casualties of this war are wayward Christians, who like Lot, let the world consume them. Though we know from Scripture that God saved Lot (2 Peter 2:7–8 tells us that God rescued "righteous Lot"), Abram's nephew did not put on the full armor of God and stand firm against the schemes of the devil (Ephesians 6:11).

This is why those in a life of faith must get involved. This is where spiritual people must be concerned for those who have gone astray from the family of faith. This involvement in spiritual warfare is demonstrated by Abram's involvement in hand-to-hand combat with the ungodly kings.

The Contribution (vv. 13–16)

Abram has not been mentioned in this story up to this point, but we see his involvement beginning in verse 13. "Then a fugitive came and told Abram the Hebrew. Now he was living by the oaks of Mamre the Amorite." Abram had not moved since he and Lot separated for the sake of peace. He was exactly where God wanted him to be. He was comfortable and things were peaceable because Abram made allies with those around him. But his peaceable and comfortable situation was about to change.

God, in his providence, had someone escape so that Abram could know about the battle, the casualties, and especially the fact that the four kings had taken his nephew Lot captive. The news brought to Abram would be a test of Abram's faith. Abram now had to make a decision. Was he going to get involved in world affairs or was he going to isolate himself?

Abram could very well have rationalized away his involvement in this matter. In regard to helping the five kings he could have said, "You know, that king of Sodom is an ungodly man. In fact, Sodom and Gomorrah is filled with sinners. They are only getting what they deserve." In regard to his own nephew he could have said, "Lot made his own decision; he deserves what he is getting. He did not give me one thought when I gave him the choice. It serves him right." Abram could have rationalized staying out of the matter, but he chose not to.

He realized that the life of faith does not mean isolation from the world, nor does it mean identification with the world. Abram understood that if he was going to be the blessing bearer to the world, if he was going to declare the truth of the one true God, he was going to have to get involved. Paraphrased, Jesus put it this way, "Be in the world, but not of the world" (John 17:14ff). That would be the balance that Abram would have to find.

After the news of the conquest of the four kings, Abram, moved by his love for his nephew and his desire to be involved with world affairs for God's glory, went into action. We are told in verses 14–15, "When Abram heard that his relative had been taken captive, he led out his trained men, born in his house, three hundred and eighteen, and went in pursuit as far as Dan. He divided his forces against them by night, he and his servants, and defeated them, and pursued them as far as Hobah, which is north of Damascus."

Abram got involved in the battle for the sake of the casualties. In doing so he gathered three hundred and eighteen men from within his house. At first one may think that three hundred and eighteen is not very many, and it's not—if the one you are fighting has more. But the number of men that came from Abram's house gives an indication that Abram was prospering. To have three hundred and eighteen servants in one house is impressive.

We can only speculate on how many troops the four kings had, but one could speculate that they had quite a few. The number of men that Abram brought may well have been fewer than the ones they were fighting, but the fact that they surprised them by night and that God was on their side enabled them to have victory of the four kings, "He brought back all the goods, and also brought back his relative Lot with his possessions, and also the women, and the people."

Abram's concern went beyond his nephew Lot; he was also concerned about all the people who were subjugated to the unjust rule of the four kings. Abram understood that being the blessing bearer and a witness for the one true God meant he had to be in the world, but not of the world. He understood that he had the responsibility of declaring the righteousness and the salvation of God, and to do this he had to be involved.

Those who live a life of faith today are in a battle, a spiritual battle, one that we must be involved in. We must avoid isolating ourselves from the world. Yes, there are sinners out there, and yes, there are ungodly people out there, but these are not the enemy, they are the casualties of the war. They need a witness of the righteousness, hope, and salvation of God found only in the person of Jesus Christ. God accomplishes his will by using his people, as they get involved in the spiritual battle.

Our Lord gave us marching orders when he said, "You shall love the Lord your God with all your heart … and your neighbor as yourself (Luke 10:27)" and "Go therefore and make disciples of all nations, baptizing them in the name of the Father, and the Son, and the Holy Spirit, teaching them to observe all that I have commanded" (Matthew 28:19–20). To love our neighbor as ourselves means that we will get involved in the spiritual battle because we don't want our neighbors to be casualties of the war. To go and make disciples of all nations means that we get involved for the purpose of saving people from destruction.

God's people must step into spiritual warfare by using the weapons of truth and righteousness, by advancing the kingdom of God through the proclamation of the gospel of Jesus Christ, and by standing up for righteousness and justice. God's people can do this only by getting involved in the battle. The life of faith is a life of war. Another truth that we see in this Genesis 14 concerning spiritual warfare is the truth concerning the attitude for spiritual warfare.

The Attitude for Spiritual Warfare (vv. 17–20)

After the defeat of the four kings, Abram would encounter two kings. The arrival of the two kings brought spiritual opposites. One king ruled over the excessively sinful city Sodom. The other king of righteousness reigned over the city called Salem, which means "peace."

The Arrival of Spiritual Opposites

The arrival of the two spiritual opposites is stated starting in verse 17, "Then after his return from the defeat of Chedorlaomer and the kings who were with him, the king of Sodom went out to meet him in the valley of Shaveh (that is, the King's Valley). And Melchizedek king of Salem brought out bread and wine; now he was a priest of God Most High."

As was stated earlier these two kings were spiritual opposites. Sodom ruled an ungodly city, a city that would eventually be destroyed on the basis of God's judgment, but Melchizedek is quite the antithesis. The very name

Melchizedek[66] means "king of righteousness" or "my righteous king." He ruled over Salem, which many people believe was Jerusalem. Melchizedek suddenly just showed up on the scene. The Bible records no genealogy. But the text does tell us that he was a "priest of God Most High." It is in the blessing that Melchizedek gives to Abram that we see the source of the victory of Abram's battle and also the source of the victory of the spiritual battle.

The Source of Spiritual Victory

It is important that we understand what the blessing of Melchizedek means, because it is central to understanding the whole chapter.[67] The blessing is set forth in verses 19 and 20, "He blessed him and said, 'Blessed be Abram of God Most High, possessor of heaven and earth; and blessed be God Most High who has delivered your enemies into your hand.' " The blessings that are given are both outward and upward.[68]

The outward blessing is directed toward Abram when he says, "Blessed be Abram of God Most High." Abram is blessed because he belongs to God, because he bears the name of the one true God. The upward blessing is directed toward the Lord, "Blessed be God Most High who has delivered your enemies into your hands." Melchizedek had the proper perspective concerning Abram and his defeat. He understood that the source of Abram's victory was "God Most High, possessor of heaven and earth."[69] The Hebrew word "El-Elyon" which we translate "God Most

---

[66]This is the first mention of a priest in the Bible. Melchizedek is mentioned again about 900 years later in Psalm 110, and then another 1,000 years later in the book of Hebrews. There is much scholarly debate on whether Melchizedek was the pre-incarnate Christ or a type of Christ; however, for the purpose of our study, we'll discuss Melchizedek only in the context of Abram's life.
[67]Ross 302.
[68]Hamilton 412.
[69]Hamilton. 412.

High" refers to the superiority of God. The phrase "possessor of heaven and earth" refers to God being owner not only of Abram's plunder, but also of all creation.[70]

What do we understand from this blessing about the whole fourteenth chapter of Genesis? We learn from Melchizedek that what Abram experienced was only realized because the "God Most High, possessor of heaven and earth" empowered Abram to win this great victory.[71]

Abram responded to this blessing by tithing his plunder as an act of honor toward God who empowered him to be victorious. Abram's tithe was a declaration of trust in the Lord as well as an acknowledgement that the source of his victory was the Lord. The source of all spiritual victory is the Lord and it's important that God's people cultivate this attitude so we remain totally dependent on the Lord.

In *Experiencing God*, Henry Blackaby tells the story of how he and about two thousand other churches in Vancouver's Baptist Association were convinced that the Lord wanted them to reach the more than twenty-two million people who would come to the World Expo Fair in 1986. They began making the plans two years before the fair. The budget of the association, two years before the fair, totaled nine thousand dollars. For the year of the fair, they set the budget for over two hundred thousand dollars. They had gained commitments that would cover thirty-five percent; the remaining sixty-five percent would have to come though prayer. The whole association prayed fervently for the Lord to provide what they needed. By the end of the first year the Lord had provided two hundred and sixty-four thousand dollars. The outreach at the fair that year brought twenty thousand professions of faith. Blackaby said, "You cannot explain it except in terms of God's intervention. Only God could have done what was done."

---

[70]Hartley 150.
[71]Hartley 150.

This is true of all spiritual victory; only God can bring the victory. And it is paramount that the life of faith cultivates such an attitude for spiritual warfare. God's people involved in spiritual warfare must say with Zechariah 4:6, "Not by might nor by power, but by my Spirit, says the Lord of hosts."

Abram was granted great victory because the Lord empowered him to defeat the powerful kings, but the battle was not over. A test of faith would come to Abram, one that could bring defeat if he did not pass the test, one that reveals the temptation within spiritual warfare.

The Temptation within Spiritual Warfare

The most vulnerable time for believers in spiritual warfare is immediately after great victories won by the Lord. This was the case with Joshua after the triumph over Jericho. In Joshua 6, we learn that God gave the Israelites great victory, but in Joshua 7 we read that they were defeated.

Elijah is another example of this truth. In 1 Kings 18, Elijah was victorious on Mount Carmel, but soon after that victory, he ran for his life, afraid of what Jezebel would do with him. Again, the reason for such collapse of faith on Elijah's part is that God's people are most vulnerable to temptation after great victories won by God.

The late preacher Andrew Bonar understood this when he said, "Let us be as watchful after the victory as before the battle."[72] And what is true of Joshua and Elijah is going to be true of Abram. After this great victory that the Lord gave him, Abram is going to be vulnerable and tempted.

---

[72]Wiersbe 37.

The Temptation Presented (v. 21)

We see the temptation presented in verse 21, "The king of Sodom said to Abram, 'Give the people to me and take the goods for yourself.' " The proposition from the king of Sodom at first glance seems proper in light of what Abram just did for the five kings. It was usual that the defeating general got the spoils of the war and for the people to go back to the king who was rescued. But within this offer was a subtle temptation, a temptation of compromise. Yet unlike his time in Egypt, Abram would now pass the test and avoid the temptation.

The Test Passed (vv. 22–24)

Abram responded to the king of Sodom, "I have sworn to the Lord God Most High, possessor of heaven and earth, that I will not take a thread or a sandal thong or anything that is yours for fear you would say, 'I have made Abram rich.' I will take nothing except what the young men have eaten, and the share of the men who went with me, Aner, Eshcol, and Mamre; let them take their share." Abram's response reveals that he was learning to trust the Lord rather than to manipulate circumstances for his own gain.

Abram made an oath with the Lord of no-compromise. Although he deserved the spoils from the fight, Abram recognized that the spoils were not from the Lord and that to take them would compromise the Lord's honor as well has his total trust in God.

The actions of Abram in these verses are completely different than those he chose in Genesis 12:16. In Egypt Abram had no problem receiving the goods Pharaoh gave him. Why such different actions? In Egypt Abram had compromised his faith, but Abram had learned his lesson and therefore, before he was tempted again, he made an oath to the Lord of no-compromise when tempted by the things of this world. If Abram were going to be involved instead of remaining isolated, he had to be indifferent to the ways of the world. The only way Abram could be in the world, but not of the world was by making an oath of no-compromise.

A few years ago, before my wife and I had children, some dear friends of ours took us on a trip to Colorado. While there we were able to visit the Continental Divide, a ridge of mountains that separate streams that flow west into the Pacific Ocean from those that flow east into the Atlantic Ocean.[73] The snowcap was full of snow and it seemed that the snow was in unity, but it really was a great illusion. It was an illusion because it set on a great divide. When the snow melts in the spring, the water on the western side makes its way to the Pacific Ocean and the water on the eastern side makes its way to the Gulf of Mexico and the Atlantic Ocean. What seemed unified at one point would end up thousands of miles apart. The Continental Divide marks a dividing line.

There is a great dividing line between being in the world and living the life of faith. There is a great dividing live between being in the world, yet not being of the world. God's people have to be careful to end up on the right side of the dividing line. We have to be careful not to compromise godly principles by accommodating the prevailing culture. For when we compromise, our involvement and effectiveness in the spiritual battle is diminished.

It was A. W. Tozer who put it well when he said, "Religion today is not transforming people; rather it is being transformed by the people. It is not raising the moral level of society; it is descending to society's own level, and congratulating itself that it has scored a victory because society is smiling accepting its compromise."

There is a war taking place in every community, city, and church. A war that is global. God's spiritual people must get involved having total dependence upon the Lord who gives the

---

[73]"Continental Divide," *Microsoft Encarta 98 Encyclopedia*, CD-ROM (Microsoft Corporation, 1997).

victory, and they must do so without giving into the temptation of compromise. The casualties are too great not to get involved!

CHAPTER V:

STANDING ON THE PROMISES OF GOD

Genesis 15:1–21

Introduction

J. Hudson Taylor, the great missionary to China, traveled to a bank in England to open up an account for the China Inland Mission. While filling out the application, he came across a question asking him to designate his assets. Taylor wrote, "ten pounds and the promises of God." Hudson Taylor was a great man of faith, and the foundation for his life of faith stood on the promises of God. The promises of God are stepping-stones upon the path of life that enable his people to move forward in the life of faith.

The promises of God in Genesis 12:1–3 enabled Abram to take a step of faith toward the Promised Land. The promises of God saved Abram when he took a different path, a path that was not in line with God's plans. The promises of God gave Abram the victory over the four kings in Genesis 14, and in Genesis 15 we'll see how they enabled Abram to continue on his journey of faith.

The promises God declares in Genesis 15 are not new; rather, they are God's confirmation of promises he gave to Abram in Genesis 12. God's continuous confirmation and reassurance of his promises keep Abram going in the right direction.

Genesis 15 is a pivotal chapter both in the narrative of the life of Abram as well in the story of God's great plan of redemption for all humanity. It begins a significant transition from a focus on the Promised Land to a focus on that of the promised seed, or the heirs of Abram. Of great importance is the glimpse Genesis provides of God's unfolding plan of redemption. Genesis 15 is mentioned three times in the New Testament, twice by the apostle Paul and once by the apostle James. In all three occurrences[74] we find them defending justification by faith and expounding on the nature of true saving faith.

All those who are on the journey of faith can stand on the same promises that Abraham was able to stand on. Charles Spurgeon has rightly said that the promises of God are the Christian's "Magna Charta of liberty, they are the title deeds of his heavenly estate. They are the jewel room in which the Christian's crown treasures are preserved." The first observation that we make in Genesis 15 is that God's people stand on his supernatural promises.

Standing on God's Supernatural Promises

> After these things the word of the LORD came to Abram in a vision, saying, "Do not fear, Abram, I am a shield to you; your reward shall be very great." (Genesis 15:1)

---

[74]Romans 4:3, Galatians 3:6, James 2:23.

As I've mentioned before, God's people are most vulnerable to temptation and discouragement after great victories won by the Lord. Abram, after making a great declaration of no-compromise to the king of Sodom, would become discouraged and somewhat dismayed. After the great battle we read about in Genesis 14, God, knowing Abram's thoughts and feelings, would address them in a supernatural way, "After these things the word of the Lord came to Abram in a vision." Before we examine the nature of the word of God that came to Abram, we would do well to recognize the means by which Abram received this word.

The text tells us that the word of the Lord came to Abram "in a vision." This type of vision was one way that God's prophets would receive a word from him. The manner in which Abram received the word suggests that Abram was a prophet, a title that in Genesis 20:7 would be specifically given to Abram.[75]

In addition, the vision that brought about the word was similar to other instances in the Bible where God's word was used to bring encouragement to certain people or groups. The Lord also calms fears as well as encourages. In the New Testament three such occurrences (Acts 18:9; 23:11; 27:23) take place with the apostle Paul.[76] God's vision to Abram would come to calm his fears as well as to encourage him.

The very first thing the word of God addresses is Abram's fear, "After these things the word of the Lord came to Abram in a vision, saying, 'Do not fear.' " We can only speculate as to what caused Abram to fear. It could have been the reality of the hostility that he would have to face on his journey of faith. Perhaps while he was waiting for God to fulfill his promises, doubt and fear set in. One thing we know for sure: the Lord is going to address Abram's fears and he does so through his supernatural promises. The first promise he gives to Abram is one of supernatural protection.

---

[75]Hamilton 418.
[76]Hamilton 418.

The Promise of Supernatural Protection

The promise of supernatural protection is found in the Lord's declaration to Abram, "I am a shield to you." The Hebrew word translated here as "shield" is the same root of the Hebrew word in Genesis 14:20, which is translated "deliver." The context of the latter is when Melchizedek declared that the Lord was the one who brought Abram's deliverance from the enemy. In Genesis 15:1 the Lord confirmed his blessing upon Abram by promising him continual supernatural protection. The word translated as shield is appropriate because a warrior would carry a shield for protection. In the same manner, the Lord promises Abram that he would deliver him from the enemy, that he would be his protection in the midst of a hostile territory. Just as the Lord supernaturally protected Abram from Pharaoh, and just as the Lord supernaturally protected Abram from the power of the four kings, the Lord would continue to give Abram supernatural protection throughout his journey of faith.

King David trusted in the Lord's supernatural protection when he said in Psalm 3 that the Lord was his "shield." Likewise, when David declared in Psalm 23, "Yea though I walk through the valley of the shadow of death, I fear no evil, for you are with me, your rod and your staff they comfort me," he was declaring that the Lord would protect him with a supernatural protection.

The Promise of Supernatural Provision

The Lord also gave Abram a promise of supernatural provision in the latter part of verse 1, "Your reward shall be very great." The idea the Lord conveyed to Abram is that of "payment." This phrase is tied in with the previous chapter. It was after the blessing of Melchizedek that Abram responded by giving a tenth of all the plunder that he accumulated from the battle. By tithing on the plunder, Abram acknowledged that the Lord was truly the "possessor of heaven and earth" and that God was the source of victory.

After tithing ten percent of the plunder, the king of Sodom offered Abram all the plunder for himself; however, Abram did not accept it because he did not want to compromise his faith and bring dishonor upon the Lord.[77] The Lord affirmed to Abram that his faithfulness did not go unnoticed and that the Lord would take care of his provisions.

Some translate this verse to mean that the Lord is Abram's reward, that is, because Abram has the Lord he does not need the tainted plunder of earthly kings.[78] I would say that because Abram has the Lord as his reward, he could be sure of the Lord's provisions. Abram does not have to take tainted plunder because the Lord, the King of kings, is greater than any king, including Pharaoh or the king of Sodom. Abram did not have to compromise his faith to get ahead because the Lord would reward his faithfulness.

The apostle Paul declared this truth when he wrote, "My God will supply all your needs according to the riches in glory in Christ Jesus" (Philippians 4:19). Just as the Lord promised to reward the faithfulness of Abram, he also promises to reward the faithfulness of all his children.

The promise of supernatural provision reminds me of one of the stories that I heard while I was serving at First Baptist Church of Dallas. A woman in the church was a very generous giver to kingdom purposes. She always wore a necklace with a gold shovel pendant. She said that she wore it because it reminded her that she could never out give the Lord and that her "reward shall be very great."

Many men would have been totally satisfied with the supernatural promises of protection and provision given to Abram, but Abram wasn't. This is not to say that Abram disrespected these two great promises or that he did he not care for them. But Abram was looking for something greater—the fulfillment of the promise of a supernatural progeny.

---

[77]Hartley 155.
[78]Hamilton 419.

The Promise of a Supernatural Progeny

Up to this point we have seen monologue recorded on the part of the Lord, but now we will "listen in" on a dialogue between Abram and the Lord. Genesis 15:2 presents the first recorded conversation between God and Abram.[79] Abram responded to the Lord's promises with what seems at first like a complaint, "Abram said, 'O Lord God, what will you give me, since I am childless, and the heir of my house is Eliezer of Damascus?' " The "complaint" that Abram made is by no means from a lack of faith in God or from unbelief, rather it is a show of Abram's confidence that God would, as promised in Genesis 12 and 13, make him a "great nation"[80] and make his descendents "as the dust of the earth."[81]

In Abram's mind the promises of supernatural protection and provision meant nothing if he had no son to benefit from the inheritance. If anything, the question Abram posed arose out of trust. Abram believed the Lord would make him a great nation and make his descendants as many as the dust of the earth, but he wanted to know when and how God would fulfill his promise.

Abram and Sarai were already up there in years and, from Abram's perspective, God seemed to be taking his time in fulfilling his promise. Their biological clocks stopped ticking a long time ago and Abram thought a delay was not going to help. Cultural practices were also at the forefront of Abram's mind when he said to the Lord, "I am childless, and the heir of my household is Eliezer of Damascus." It was common practice that if there were no blood heir, the head of the household would adopt a servant in the household to be the heir.[82] But as we read further, we see that the Lord addressed Abram's concern. God

---

[79]Hamilton 419.
[80]Waltke 241.
[81]Genesis 13:16.
[82]Walton and Matthews 41.

revealed how he would bring about the fulfillment of his promise, and then he illustrated the magnitude of the promise.

First the Lord addressed the "how." "Then behold, the word of the Lord came to him, saying, 'This man will not be your heir; but *one who will come forth from your own body*" (Genesis 15: 4, emphasis added). The Lord told Abram to have no doubt about how he would bring about this promised seed. Though Abram and Sarai were childless, God would bring through them a promised descendent.

To be without a child in Abram's day had different connotations than it does today. In Bible times, people thought being childless was a sign of God's judgment from their wickedness. But in Abram's case it was an opportunity for God to show his supernatural power. Abram and Sarai were both well past childbearing years and the prospect of having a child eluded them long ago, but God would use their childlessness as an opportunity to show his power. The Lord would use his supernatural power to turn Abram and Sarai's hopeless situation into one filled with hope.

The Lord confirmed his promise of a supernatural progeny with a sign in verse 5, a sign that showed the magnitude of God's promise, "And he took Abram outside and said, 'Now look toward the heavens, and count the stars, if you are able to count them.' And he said to him, 'so shall your descendants be. "

Obviously, from this verse we learn that Abram's vision came to him while he was in his house. The Lord took Abram outside to look into the sky and count the stars. Imagine Abram's thoughts as God revealed the enormity of his promise in this great object lesson. The first time the Lord reaffirmed his promise to Abram he had him look down to the ground and count the dust. Some say that this was to reaffirm the Lord's commitment to give Abram the land. This time the Lord had Abram look up to the stars.

Most likely the use of "stars" to reaffirm the promise is pointing back to Abram's earlier declaration in Genesis 14:22 when he said to the king of Sodom, "I have sworn to the Lord,

God Most High, possessor of heaven and earth." To declare God to be possessor of heaven and earth pointed to the creative power of God. It was God's creative power that made the heavens and the earth, and it will be God's supernatural, creative power that would enable Abram to have descendants that outnumber the dust of the earth and the stars of the sky. Just as the Lord was faithful in his supernatural and creative power in the past, he would also be faithful to demonstrate this power in Abram's future.[83]

Abram could stand on the Lord's supernatural promises of protection, provision, and progeny. In the same way, we who are living the life of faith can stand on the promises of God, knowing that the all-powerful God who made the heavens and earth will uphold his promises.

When we claim a promise such as the one given in Isaiah 41:10, "Fear not, for I am with you. Be not dismayed for I am your God; I will strengthen you, yes, I will help you, I will uphold you with my righteous right hand," God's people can be assured that an all-powerful, supernatural God will keep that promise because of his supernatural power. Not only do we stand on God's supernatural promises, but we also stand on God's saving promises.

Standing on God's Saving Promises

> Then he believed in the LORD; and He reckoned
> it to him as righteousness. (Genesis 15:6)

Abram will respond to the Lord's reaffirmation of his promise in verse 6. We find that this was a saving response to God's promise. It is important that we understand before we get into this verse the importance it plays in God's unfolding plan of redemption and justification before God by faith alone. This great

---

[83]Sailhamer 151.

verse is used in the New Testament to teach how one is saved, by faith *alone*. That is why I call it Abram's saving response to God's promise.

The Response to God's Saving Promise

"Then he believed in the Lord"(Genesis 15:6). This declaration is a transition statement for the whole chapter, showing us the response to the first appearance that Abram had with God in this chapter and preparing us for a second appearance (which might never have happened had Abram responded differently).

To say that Abram believed the Lord in this verse is not to say that this is the first time Abram had faith in the Lord, for it was by faith that Abram left his home of Ur and traveled to the Promised Land. Abram's faith had been demonstrated by his actions, that is, by his obedience to the word of the Lord. We need to view Genesis 15:6 not as Abram's initial step of faith, but instead as his response to the supernatural promise of God reaffirmed in the first five verses of Genesis 15.

This is the first time the word "believed" is used in the Bible. It is the Hebrew word "amen." The idea conveyed by this word is that of certainty. Faith is not something that we deem possible or hopeful, but instead, biblical faith means to believe with total firmness and certainty in the object of belief.[84] This invites the question concerning that which Abram believes with certainty. In what did Abram place his total trust concerning the Lord's supernatural promises?

From the immediate text we can conclude that Abram believed the Lord would protect him, provide for him, and ultimately give him a child. All of these promises are directly related to the promises given to Abram back in Genesis 12. His belief revealed in Genesis 15 is connected more with the supernatural progeny than with anything else, and it is connected

---

[84]Gleason L. Archer, Jr., R. Laird Harris, and Bruce K. Waltke, *Theological Workbook of the Old Testament* (Chicago: Moody Press, 1980) 51.

with the promises to become a great nation and to have descendants that outnumber the dust of the earth and the stars of the heavens. If all we had was the book of Genesis, we could conclude that this is exactly what Abram "believed in the Lord." But the New Testament, especially the teachings of Paul found in the book of Galatians, gives us greater insight into exactly what Abram believed.

In Galatians 3 we see three indications of exactly what Abram believed here in Genesis 15. First, Paul told us that Abram believed in the gospel, "The Scripture, foreseeing that God would justify the Gentiles by faith, preached the gospel before hand to Abraham, saying, 'All the nations will be blessed in you' " (Galatians 3:8). Paul pointed back to God's promise of Genesis 12 and declared that Abram understood the statement, "All nations will be blessed in you" as more than a physical blessing, but rather as the greatest spiritual blessing of all, salvation.[85]

Second, we learn from the third chapter of Galatians that Abram believed in redemption. According to verses 10 through 14, Paul declared that Christ redeemed us from the curse of sin. This was done in Christ Jesus, who as Paul says "is the blessing of Abraham." Christ made the payment that set us free from the penalty and the power of sin. Abraham believed in God's redemption.[86]

Third, we learn from the teachings of Paul that Abraham believed in Christ. Paul points to this truth in Galatians 3:16 when he wrote, "Now the promises were spoken to Abraham and to his seed. He does not say, 'And to seeds,' as referring to many, but rather to one, 'And to your seed,' that is, Christ."

If we go back to the book of Genesis we can confirm that Paul is referring to the use of the Hebrew word translated "descendants" or "seed." The literal translation is the singular form of the word "seed." Paul explained that Abraham

---

[85]Boice 549.
[86]Boice 549.

understood this promise as more than just a promise of many descendants, but as a promise of one particular descendant—the Redeemer Jesus Christ—who would bring justification from sin to the whole world.[87]

Abram believed in God's good news, in God's redemption, and in a specific descendant who would bring salvation and justification. Did he understand the promise fully? No! But what he did understand completely is that he believed in the Lord. This was Abram's saving response to God's saving promise, which brought about a saving result.

The Result of God's Saving Promise

The result of Abram's belief in God's supernatural promise is declared in the latter part of verse 6, "and He reckoned it to him as righteousness." There are two words we need to understand in the saving result of God's promise: reckoned and righteousness.

As Abram placed his faith in the gospel, in redemption, and in the coming of a particular descendant whom we know as Christ, and God "reckoned it to him as righteousness." The word "reckoned" has the connotation of crediting or paying something to someone's account. The Lord imputed righteousness to Abram's account on the basis of his faith.

Some say that "righteousness" refers to Abram's act of faith, that is, his act of faith is an act of righteousness, and to some degree it is. But, what this verse means is that when Abram believed in the promise given to him about a particular seed, a seed that would bring eternal blessings, the Lord enabled Abram to have a right standing before God.

Since the fall of humanity recorded in Genesis 3, man has been condemned before God, objects of his wrath. The question that has been asked throughout the ages is, How can a person be righteous before God? Some argue that good works will give a

---

[87]Boice 550.

person right standing before God, but the Bible clearly says, "All have sinned and fall short of the glory of God" (Romans 3:23). No matter how good our works are before God, our works of righteousness are as filthy rags before a perfect God (Isaiah 64:6).

Only God can make a person righteous before him. Only God can give a person right standing before him. The way God made this possible is through the seed of Abram, who is Christ. Christ took upon himself our sin and has given us his righteousness (2 Corinthians 5:21). The only way that we can have righteousness credited to our account is through faith in God's provision of salvation. For Abram, his faith was in the promise of salvation, but for you and me our salvation is in the fulfillment of that promise, the fulfillment being Christ.

Abram demonstrated a great theological truth, a truth that Paul declared in Ephesians 2:8–9 when he said, "For by grace you have been saved, through faith; and that not of yourselves, it is the gift of God; not as a result of works, so that no one may boast." The only way one can truly have salvation, the only way one can have a right standing before God is by standing on God's saving promise of salvation in Christ. And the way that we stand on that promise is with a confident trust, not a probable trust, not a hopeful trust, but a certain trust that Christ and Christ alone is our salvation. One of the hymns of the faith describes this truth well.

> My hope is built on nothing less
> Than Jesus' blood and righteousness;
> I dare not trust the sweetest frame,
> But wholly lean on Jesus' name.
>
> When he shall come with trumpet sound,
> Oh may I then in Him be found;
> Dressed in his righteousness alone,
> Faultless to stand before the throne.

On Christ the solid Rock I stand;
All other ground is sinking sand,
All other ground is sinking sand.[88]

Any other promise of salvation is no promise at all; it is sinking sand. Abram was standing on the Lord's supernatural promises, the Lord's saving promises, and the Lord's sure promises.

Standing on God's Sure Promises

After Abram demonstrated his certain belief in the promise of eternal life, the Lord would then make a sure covenant with Abram, a covenant that came only after Abram placed his total trust in the Lord's saving promise.

The Sure Covenant of God

The covenant that is made in the next verse is one primarily concerning the land the Lord promised to Abram and his descendants, but it is also a covenant that guaranteed the Lord's fulfillment of both the promise of land and seed.

The Lord said to Abram in verse 7, "I am the Lord who brought you out of Ur of the Chaldeans, to give you this land to possess it." Here the Lord reaffirmed the promise of land to Abram, and Abram responded in verse 8, "How may I know that I will possess it." Abram believed, but he needed a little help with his faith. In giving Abram help, the Lord made a covenant with Abram, as we'll read in the verses that follow.

This is not the first time we read of a covenant in Genesis. The Lord made a covenant with Noah in Genesis 6 and with all humanity in Genesis 9, right after the flood. This next covenant

---

[88] "My Hope Is Built on Nothing Less," words by Edward Mote, circa 1834; music by William B. Bradbury, 1863, verses 1 and 4 and refrain.

the Lord made dealt with Abram's physical descendants and applies in a secondary manner to Abram's spiritual descendants, those of us who have placed our faith in Christ Jesus.[89]

Covenants were very common in the ancient Near East. They were made between parties for the purpose of defining the nature of the relationship that was being entered into. The covenant defined the responsibilities and the obligations of both the parties entering into covenant together.[90] But the covenant the Lord made with Abram was different. It was one-sided. God gave the directions to Abram concerning the covenant in verses 9 through 11, telling him to gather animals for sacrifice. The Lord then prophesied concerning the future of Abram's descendants and how they would suffer under Egyptian bondage and how the Lord would deliver them to back to the Promised Land. After he prophesied, the Lord ratified the covenant, "It came about when the sun had set, that it was very dark, and behold, there appeared a smoking oven and a flaming torch which passed between these pieces" (v. 17). The Lord passed through the animal pieces that Abram had cut.

Normally, a covenant like this would require that Abram pass between the cut-up animals; however, it is significant that Abram did not have to pass through. This one-sided covenant was not dependent upon Abram, but upon the Lord himself. The sure covenant of God was based upon the sure character of God.

The Sure Character of God

The covenant was dependent upon God's grace and upon God's character. Though potentially Abram would fail at times to fulfill his covenant obligations, the Lord would never fail his. That is why the Lord told Abram that he could be sure that after Egypt he would bring Abram back to his land; God would uphold his end of the covenant. And just as the Lord has been faithful

---

[89]Boice 561–562.
[90]Hartley 157–158.

throughout history to his covenant with Abram, Christians can be assured that the Lord is always faithful to his promises. For the eternal covenant that the Lord made is made not with the blood of animals, but with the precious blood of Jesus Christ (1 Peter 1:18–19). God's promises are sure because they are not based on what we do, but on who God is.

What promises are you standing on? The only sure promises to stand on are the Lord's supernatural and saving promises. The only way we can stand on those promises is through total trust in Christ Jesus. If you stand on anything else, you are on sinking sand.

CHAPTER VI:

THE WAITING IS THE HARDEST PART

Genesis 16:1–16

Introduction

If you live in Dallas, one of the "privileges" you have is dealing with the enormous traffic problem. I was reminded of this problem recently when I took a day trip there. To make matters worse, it rained on the day I went.

That particular day the traffic seemed to be bumper to bumper and I never got over forty miles per hour. Needless to say, I grew impatient. I gripped the steering wheel waiting for something to happen, waiting for someone to move. I was frustrated because I had a destination in mind, but it seemed as though I would never get there.

My story illustrates a well-known fact about human nature: we don't like to wait. We have fast-food restaurants because we don't like to wait, and we'll avoid sit-down restaurants if the line is too long.

The ABC show 20/20 once aired an experiment with children on waiting and self-control. The children were given two choices: they could have a cookie right away or they could wait while the reporter ran an errand and then they could have two cookies. Some of the preschoolers grabbed the single cookie immediately, while others waited up to twenty minutes to receive their two cookies. Those who wanted the two cookies used all kinds of tactics to sustain themselves. Some covered their eyes so they would not see the cookies set before them. Some rested their heads on their arms, talked to themselves, sang, and even tried to sleep. The follow-up of this study revealed that those who were able to wait and forgo the instant gratification kept that same temperament throughout their adolescence. The more impulsive kids, those who gave into instant gratification, grew up to be more stubborn, indecisive, and stressed.

In the life of faith, waiting on God is the hardest part. Just as we dislike waiting at restaurants, in lines, and in traffic, we also dislike waiting on God to act on our behalf. It is not that we don't want God to act; it is just that we want him to act on our behalf according to our timing, not his. We know that God wants to teach us patience, but we want him to hurry up and do it. In Genesis 16 we see Abram and Sarai struggling with waiting on God. They are growing impatient. In Abram and Sarai's growing impatience we see why the waiting is the hardest part.

The Waiting Is the Hardest Part

Genesis 16:1 shows that Abram and Sarai are in God's waiting room, "Now Sarai, Abram's wife had borne him no children." We started our study in the last part of Genesis 11 where we were told that Sarai was barren. Yet God had promised Abram that he would be a "great nation" and that his descendants would outnumber the dust of the earth and the stars of the heavens, but still they had no child. Abram and Sarai were in God's waiting room, in God's holding pattern. Genesis 16:3 tells us they had been in this pattern for ten years. This was the ten-year time period between God's promise of a child (Genesis 11 and 12) and their current situation (Genesis 16). They had been waiting for God to fulfill his promise of a seed for a decade.

From Genesis 15, we remember that Abram wondered how God would fulfill his promise when he asked the Lord if it would be Eliezer, his servant, who would be the heir, and the Lord told him that Abram's heir would be from his own body.

Now the Lord never specifically said that the seed would come through both Abram and Sarai, but it sure is implied in verse 16:1 where the narrative says that Sarai was Abram's wife. This designation of Sarai as Abram's wife points us back to Genesis 2 where we see God creating the institution of marriage—a man shall leave his father and mother and become one flesh with his wife. God's creative intention is that there be one man and one woman in marriage and that procreation would take place through this institution.

The scene is set. We find Abram and Sarai in God's waiting room, longing for God to fulfill his promise. But the waiting is the hardest part, and during that time we are often tempted to question God's timing and ability in our situation when he seems to be doing nothing about it.

We Are Tempted to Question God's Timing and Ability in our Situation

We are told in verse 1 that not only was Sarai childless, but also that she had a maid whose name was Hagar. Hagar is an important character in Genesis 16, one that we will see more of in following verses.

After the setting of the scene in verse 1, the author reveals that Sarai is beginning to question God's timing and ability in this situation, "So Sarai said to Abram, 'Now behold, the Lord has prevented me from bearing children.' " To some degree Sarai is right about the Lord preventing her from bearing a child, but she is not making a statement of fact; instead she is complaining and even blaming God for her childless situation. We need to recognize Sarai's frustration, which is directed toward the Lord.

When Sarai was promised a child she was no spring chicken, but now, some ten years has passed and it is very possible that menopause had set in, eliminating any human possibility for her to have a child. Therefore she directed her frustration with the Lord to Abram. Sarai questioned not only God's promise, but also his character. This is the temptation that can arise when we are in God's waiting room, a temptation that is presented before us from the Devil himself.

What took place in Genesis 16 parallels what happened in Genesis 3. When the serpent (the Devil) tempted Eve, he did so with questions about God's truthfulness and God's character. The Devil was at it once again; he wanted Sarai to give into the temptation and to question God's timing and ability.

The Devil had a vested interest in tempting Sarai. You have to remember that the Lord sentenced the Devil to ultimate defeat back in Genesis 3 when he said that the seed of the woman would crush the seed of the serpent. This was an indication of the Devil's ultimate doom, a doom that would come through the seed of the woman, through the seed of Abraham, and that was sealed by the person of Jesus Christ. The Devil did not want the promised child to come about because he did not want to meet his ultimate destiny of destruction.

In the same way that the Devil tried to thwart the plan of God's unfolding redemption, he also tries to thwart God's plans for our lives when we are waiting on God to act on our behalf. In thwarting that plan he will tempt us so that we will begin to question God's timing and ability.

It is important to note that even after Genesis 16 and all that takes place in it, Sarai will still have to wait about another fifteen years to see the promise of a child fulfilled. The reason for the long wait is that God wants Abram and Sarai to be in a situation where only God's ability and power could bring about the fulfillment of the promise.

Similar temptations take place with people who sign up for short-term mission trips. They put their name down to go even though they don't have the money. They make their needs known, but the money does not come. They begin to question God's timing and ability almost to the point of backing out. I tell people like that to wait because the Devil wants to keep people from going to share the gospel, but God likes to get us to where we know without a doubt that he, and he alone, provides.

If we fail to overcome the temptation of questioning God's timing and ability, it can lead us to more troubles. When we get frustrated with God, then we are tempted to look to the world for solutions to our situation.

We Are Tempted to Look to the World for Solutions

That is exactly what Sarai did. Past the point of no return, she let the temptation of the Devil cast doubt about the Lord and seduce her senses, and with this she would now look to the world for a solution to her situation.

Sarai had a plan, a worldly strategy, but at least she could see something in action. That seemed more than what God was doing at this point. Sarai devised her own plot with her maid Hagar and Abram as the main characters, "Please go into my maid; perhaps I will obtain children through her" (Genesis 16:2). You can see her thinking at this point, "God gives us the ability to make decisions and act on them, so maybe he's waiting for me to do something." At this point, Sarai, like Eve, decided to be like God and help him out with fulfilling his promise. But in reality she resorted to a human solution to a divine situation.

What Sarai proposed was a regular and accepted practice in her culture. If the wife was barren, it was not uncommon for the husband to take another wife for the purpose of having children. We should not think it too odd; it is similar to our having surrogate mothers today. But the reality of this solution is that it was a worldly way out.

Further evidence this was a worldly resolution is found in the fact that Hagar was an Egyptian. Most likely, Abram and Sarai attained Hagar during their journey into Egypt, a journey they took because Abram, instead of waiting on God, looked to the world for solutions. Also, you may remember that for the most part when God's people went to Egypt they did so because they were not trusting in the Lord, but looking to the world for solutions. That is what Sarai did; she looked to the world instead of waiting on the Lord.

What may seem to be an acceptable practice to the world may not be from the Lord. The Lord intended for man to be married to one woman and to have children with his wife. Thus, the world may accept a common solution to a situation, but that does not mean that it is God's will. Yet we are quick to act on our own, as evidenced by Abram's response to Sarai's suggestion. Here, Abram reveals one more temptation: when waiting on God we listen to other voices for our supervision.

We Are Tempted to Listen to Other Voices for Our Supervision

Sarai told Abram the plan and then he responded, "And Abram listened to the voice of Sarai." (Genesis 16:2). Who did Abram listen to? He listened to his wife. This is exactly what happened in Genesis 3 with Adam; he listened to the voice of Eve. In both instances the husbands relinquished their responsibility of leadership by listening to the voices of their wives when they should have listened to the voice of God. In Adam's case he should have remembered that the Lord told him personally not to eat of the tree. In Abram's case he should have told Sarai that the Lord promised him in a vision a child through Abram and his God-ordained wife. Don't get me wrong; sometimes it is wise for husbands to listen to their wives, but never in disobedience to

God's word, which is the context of Adam and Abram's situations.

When we are in God's holding pattern, we will begin to hear many voices, voices of doubt, temptation, and despair, voices with worldly solutions. But the one voice we must listen to is that of the Lord. Waiting on God is the hardest part because we are often tempted to question God's timing and ability, to look to the world for solutions, and to listen to those whose counsel is not godly. When we give into these temptations instead of waiting on God, we will find that the troubles we are trying solve will not depart.

The Troubles Will Not Depart

Sarai might have had good intentions when she took things into her own hands, but her plans would cause problems. When Sarai and Abram tried to solve a divine situation with a human solution, they learned two lessons. First, they learned that when you fail to wait on God and resort to human solutions, troubles are not solved; instead, they become worse.

Human Solutions Can Make Troubles Worse

In verses 3 through 6 Sarai and Abram resorted to the human solution for fulfilling God's divine plan, "After Abram had lived ten years in the land of Canaan, Abram's wife Sarai took Hagar the Egyptian, her maid, and gave her to her husband as his wife." This designation of Hagar as "Abram's wife" elevated Hagar from her lowly position as Sarai's servant to being her equal. The change in status also shows a transfer of authority and responsibility. Hagar was previously Sarai's responsibility, but now she would be Abram's responsibility.[91]

---

[91]Hartley 165.

Verse 4 tells us that Abram and Sarai had relations and that Hagar conceived. Their plan was successful. Or was it? Sarai would soon find out that in addition to this not solving her infertility problem, she had made things worse.

Hagar, enjoying her elevated status and the fact that she was carrying Abram's child, let pride take over. "He went into Hagar, and she conceived; and when she saw that she had conceived, her mistress was despised in her sight." Hagar had an attitude problem. We are told that she despised Sarai in her sight. The Hebrew word translated "despised" in this verse is the same root of the Hebrew word translated "curse" in Genesis 12:3 where the Lord promises Abram that he will curse those who curse Abram. Hagar showed great disrespect and dishonor toward her former mistress. Not only did that make things worse between Hagar and Sarai, but it also caused problems between husband and wife.

The once quiet and peaceful home was now a battlefield with Hagar despising Sarai, Sarai in turn despising Hagar, and now Sarai blaming Abram for Hagar's attitude, "And Sarai said to Abram, 'May the wrong done me be upon you. I gave my maid into your arms, but when she saw that she had conceived, I was despised in her sight. May the Lord judge between you and me." Sarai, in so many words, attacked Abram and blamed him for her problems. Isn't that just like human nature? Instead of taking responsibility for our own sins we blame others.

Abram would respond by once again acquiescing to his wife instead of assuming leadership, "But Abram said to Sarai, 'Behold, your maid is in your power; do to her what is good in your sight." Abram put Hagar back under the power and responsibility of Sarai by moving Hagar back to her servant position.

Sarai would use her rank to get back at Hagar, "So Sarai treated her harshly, and she fled from her presence." The word "harshly" is the same word used to describe the treatment of the Israelites when they were in bondage in Egypt. Hagar received treatment so cruel that she had to flee from Abram's home.

The human solution to a divine promise did not work out. Things got terribly worse within the household of Abram. Disunity as well as abuse plagued the home. Why? Human solutions often intensify troubles. One person has rightly said, "In whatever man does without God, he must fail miserably, or succeed more miserably."[92] Though the conception might have seemed like a successful solution to their problem, their troubles multiplied—and they became permanent.

Human Solutions Can Make Troubles Permanent

After Hagar fled, she made her way into the wilderness and stopped by a spring on the way to Shur. It is by this spring that Hagar would have an encounter with the angel of the Lord. The appearing of the angel of the Lord is what theologians call a theophany. In this theophany we see God address Hagar's affliction. What took place between the Lord and Hagar demonstrates the concern God has for all people. Abram was God's chosen man, but God was and is still concerned for those (like Hagar) outside the covenant.

The Lord would take care of Hagar and her child; however, another gross effect of Sarai and Abram's human intervention would result in Hagar's son Ishmael becoming a permanent problem for the nation of Israel. In Genesis 16:10, the Lord told Hagar that he would "greatly multiply her descendants, so that they will be too many to count." The angel of the Lord went on to say, "Behold, you are with child, and you will bear a son; and you shall call his name Ishmael, because the Lord has given heed to your affliction. He will be a wild donkey of a man, his hand will be against everyone, and everyone's hand will be against him; and he will live to the east of his brothers" (Genesis 16:11–12). Ishmael's future would be characterized by hostility.

---

[92]Wiersbe 56.

To be a "wild donkey" means to be in constant conflict. Ishmael and his descendants would always be in conflict with Abram's promised child, Isaac.

Even today, looking at the relations between the Middle East and Israel, we witness the enduring and permanent nature of the problem that Sarai and Abram created by resorting to their own solution. Despite the great deal of talk about peace in the Middle East and between the Israelis and Arabs, it will truly never happen because the Lord says here that there will be constant conflict between Ishmael and his half brother Isaac. Every time you read about an explosion in Israel or about Israel attacking the Palestinians, remember that the conflict is the fruit of not waiting on God.

How can we avoid making mistakes like Abram and Sarai? How can we keep ourselves from the temptation to act on our circumstances while we should be waiting on God? The answer is found in the heart.

The Answer Is in the Heart

Let's examine the dialogue in Genesis 16 between the Lord and Hagar. In this discourse the Lord reveals a truth that Abram and Sarai knew, but because of their impatience they forgot. What the Lord promised Hagar and how she responded reveals the great truth of this chapter—answers are found in who God is and can be attained only from within the heart of God's people. To wait for the Lord, not resorting to our own hasty actions, we need a heart that prays.

A Heart that Prays

The dialogue between Hagar and the Lord says nothing about prayer, but the implication exists in the name the Lord gave to Hagar's son, "Behold, you are with child, and you will bear a son; and you shall call his name Ishmael, because the Lord has given heed to your affliction." The name Ishmael means "God hears." It does not say that Hagar prayed, but we know that the Lord heard her affliction, her crying out because of the harsh treatment at the hands of her mistress Sarai.

When Hagar went back to live in the house of Abram and gave birth to the child, Abram did indeed name him Ishmael. Hagar told Abram everything the Lord told her when he appeared to her in the wilderness. Every time Abram and Sarai said the name Ishmael they would be reminded of their failure to fervently pray and wait on God instead of resorting to human devices. Too many times God's people have the attitude "when all else fails, pray." But the reality is all else will fail, unless we pray. Unfortunately, Abram and Sarai found this out the hard way.

Are you in God's waiting room? Then pray. God hears you and he understands the affliction you are in. Don't question God. Don't look to the world. Don't listen to other voices for direction. Pray fervently to the Lord, for he hears you and he sees you, he knows what you need and when you need it. Have a heart that not only prays, but that also believes.

A Heart that Believes

Genesis 16:13–14 proves that Hagar believed what the Lord told her, "Then she called the name of the Lord who spoke to her, 'You are a God who sees'; for she said, 'Have I even remained alive after seeing him?' " What a great declaration of faith and hope. She believed the promise of God, put her hope in the promise, and then made her way back to Abram and Sarai as the Lord commanded.

God puts us in his waiting room, sometimes in long holding patterns for a reason. He makes us wait so we will learn to seek him in prayer and take him at his word. He doesn't answer right away so that he can produce within us a character that perseveres. His purposeful delay helps us learn to trust in his wise and sovereign will. The more quickly we learn to submit and yield to him, the less trouble we will bring upon ourselves and the more blessings God will shower upon us.

As I was writing this section of the book, a secular song that I listened to as a teenager kept coming to my mind, *The Waiting* by Tom Petty and the Heart Breakers. The lyrics speak of a man waiting for a relationship to flower into full-blown love. But the chorus of the song can really speak to the journey of faith and walking with God. In fact, I "borrowed" words from the chorus for the title of this chapter.

> The waiting is the hardest part
> Everyday you see one more card
> You take it on faith, you take it to the heart
> The waiting is the hardest part

Certainly on the journey of faith the waiting is the hardest part. It is hard because of the temptations that will come as we wait for God to act. It is difficult because when we give into those temptations and resort to human solutions apart from God the troubles do not really depart, but often become worse and sometimes permanent. The answer for waiting is found in the heart that knows that God hears and sees, leading us to pray and believe, yielding patiently to God's wise and sovereign will.

Are you waiting on God? To give you guidance? To bring you deliverance? Pray, believe, and wait patiently because the Lord hears you and sees you. Pray and believe because "the Lord fulfills the desires of those who fear him; he hears their cry and saves them" (Psalm 145:19). Keep waiting—God will act on your behalf in his perfect timing.

CHAPTER VII:

THE COVENANT

Genesis 17:1–27

Introduction

An overriding theme from Genesis to Revelation is that of a covenant. The term covenant, as used in the Bible, describes how God relates to man. In fact, one could say that at the heart of God's plan of redemption is the notion of a covenant. At the heart of biblical history is the idea of covenant.[93]

Covenants are not exclusive to the biblical record. Studies of other ancient texts reveal that covenants permeated the ancient Near East. They were common between governments and those being governed. For example, a king would enter into a covenant with the people to regulate the behavior of both the regime and the people. The government promised to protect its citizens if the general public promised allegiance, support, and tribute to the government.[94]

---

[93]William Dyrness, *Themes in Old Testament Theology* (Downers Grove: Inter Varsity Press, 1979) 113.
[94]Dyrness 114.

In its simplest definition, a covenant is a promise between two parties that is binding by either a verbal or symbolic oath.[95] God used the idea of covenant as a means of relating to man, but he expanded on its simplest form. One characteristic particular to God's covenants with man includes the unchanging nature of a covenant. Biblical covenants may be superseded or replaced, but they cannot be changed. Throughout the Scriptures, God reveals additional details of his covenants, but one common theme runs through all of God's covenants—the unchanging truth that God declares, "I will be their God, and they shall be my people."[96] This is the heart of the covenant between God and man.

Another characteristic of God's covenants with man is that they are divinely imposed and initiated. It is God's desire to have a relationship with man, and therefore he initiates this through the concept of covenant.[97] The implication of God's covenantal relationship with man is stated early in the biblical record. The first evidence of a covenant between God and man is found in the account of the Garden of Eden before the fall (Genesis 3). God entered into a covenant with Adam. He promised to take care of and provide for Adam. All Adam had to do was to abstain from eating from one particular tree in the garden. By disobeying the Lord's command, Adam did not keep his part of the covenant.

Adam's disobedience brought death, both physical and spiritual. Sinful man is now separated from holy God, thus the relationship between the two is severed. From this point the covenant is not a covenant of works, as in Genesis 2, but a covenant of grace, a covenant that is undeserving, extended by God to sinful man only because of God's goodness.

The first implication of this covenant of grace is declared in Genesis 3:15 when the Lord says that the seed of the woman is going to crush the seed of the serpent. The Lord's covenant of

---

[95]Dyrness 114.
[96]Wayne Grudem, *Systematic Theology* (Grand Rapids: Zondervan, 1994) 515.
[97]Grudem 515.

grace is also explicitly declared between God and Noah (Genesis 6). The Lord grew weary of the sinfulness of man and no longer wanted to strive with man; therefore, he pronounced judgment upon humanity. However, this judgment did not affect Noah who found favor in the eyes of the Lord. Some say that Noah found favor because he was a righteous man, but I contend that he found favor with God through Noah's faith by God's grace, which led Noah to become a righteous man. God's covenant of grace is not based on man's goodness, but on God's.

God's covenant of grace continues to be unequivocally affirmed as well as expanded on in the life of Abraham. God called Abram from his hometown of Ur and led him to the Land of Promise. The covenant declaration in Genesis 12 is reiterated in Genesis 13 and sealed with an oath in Genesis 15. Yet, as we read in Genesis 17, the Lord continued to add details to his covenant with Abram.

But it doesn't stop in Genesis 17. Throughout the biblical record God added details to his covenant of grace through the Mosaic and Davidic covenants. Finally, God's covenant of grace comes to its fulfillment with the New Covenant, through the person of Jesus Christ.

It is important that we understand the idea and nature of God's covenants because Genesis 17 is consumed with the concept and idea of covenant. The frequency of the Hebrew word "berith" underscores the need to understand the idea of covenant within the biblical record. "Berith," used no less than thirteen times in Genesis 17, gives the picture of "cutting a covenant."

The covenant of grace between the Lord and Abram has already been cut in Genesis 15 when we find God commanding Abram to take several animals and cut them in half. After he did as the Lord said, Abram fell into a deep sleep. Then the Lord himself walked between the cut animals as a sign of his oath concerning his covenant with Abram, a covenant that dealt with both the promise of land as well as with the promise of a seed.

Now in Genesis 17 the Lord reaffirmed as well as expanded on his covenant of grace with Abram. Because in the previous chapter Abram and Sarai failed to wait on God, resorting to human solutions for a divine situation, and possibly thinking they had helped the Lord fulfill his promise, the Lord determined to confirm and develop his covenant with Abram. In doing so, we see four aspects arise out of God's covenant of grace. The first aspect is that of comfort.

A Covenant of Comfort

Genesis 17 opens by informing us that Abram was ninety-nine years old. If you look back at the last verse of Genesis 16 you read that "Abram was eighty-six years old when Hagar bore Ishmael to him." Some thirteen years had passed as Abram and Sarai waited on God. In Jewish tradition, Ishmael was now the age of manhood.

After these thirteen years, "the Lord appeared to Abram" (Genesis 17:1) and he reaffirmed and gave more detail concerning the covenant between them. In reaffirming the covenant with Abram we make three observations that reveal why entering a covenant with the Lord is a covenant of comfort. The first observation is the powerful nature of the covenant.

The Powerful Nature of the Covenant

In appearing to Abram, the Lord declared, "I am God Almighty." The Hebrew name "El-Shaddai," which is translated "God Almighty," is used here for the first time in the Bible. It is used some forty-eight times in the rest of the Old Testament.[98] Using El-Shaddai here, the Lord communicates to Abram that he is El-Shaddai, the powerful God of the universe. He reminded Abram that the one with whom Abram has a covenant relationship is the

---

[98]Walton and Matthews 43.

omnipotent and all-sufficient God who can do anything and meet any need.[99]

This reminder would bring a great deal of comfort to Abram on his journey of faith. Abram would be comforted knowing that the God who promised to make him a great nation would be able to complete it. Abram would be comforted knowing that the God who promised that his descendants would outnumber the dust of the earth and the stars of the sky would be able to fulfill it. Abram would be comforted knowing that the God who promised to be his protection and give him provisions would be able to meet his every need.

The foundation of a covenant of faith between God and man is the power of God. The fact that God is El-Shaddai, God Almighty, gives assurance to those who are in a covenant relationship with a God who will fulfill his covenant obligations. Because God is El-Shaddai, he could say with confidence, "I will establish my covenant between me and you, and I will multiply you exceedingly" (Genesis 17:2). Another observation that reveals that this is a covenant of comfort is found in the purposeful nature of the covenant.

The Purposeful Nature of the Covenant

After the Lord appeared to Abram and declared himself El-Shaddai, verse 3 details that Abram responded by falling on his face. Out of reverence, respect, and awe Abram prostrated himself before the Lord. In verse 2, the Lord reaffirmed the covenant, and then he added more detail.

The Lord said in verse 4, "As for me, behold my covenant is with you, and you will be the father of a multitude of nations." The key to this statement is the word "nations." We have already learned back in Genesis 12 that the Lord promised to make Abram into a "great nation." Here in Genesis 17, God not only

---

[99]Wiersbe 64.

reaffirmed that promise, but he also expanded it. Not only would Abram be a great nation, but also he would become the father of a multitude of nations.

How could this come about? How could Abram be the father of many nations? Sarai was still barren! Now, we must remember that the one who is expanding the covenant is El-Shaddai, God Almighty, who is all-powerful and can accomplish anything. God said twice that he would make Abram the father of a multitude of nations. He also told Abram in verse 6 that "kings will come forth from" him.

El-Shaddai would do great things through Abram and his descendants, but God revealed his power even more when he included barren Sarai in the covenant. "I will bless her, and indeed I will give you a son by her, and she shall be a mother of nations; kings of people will come from her" (Genesis 17:16). God Almighty would make Abram the father of a multitude of nations and kings would come forth from him, and all this would happen through his barren wife Sarai.

The truth of Abram being "the father of a multitude of nations" and the truth that "kings will come forth" through him is realized early in the book of Genesis. This truth is revealed in Abram's physical descendants Keturah, Ishmael, and Esau.[100] But the realization of this truth goes way beyond Genesis and Abram's physical descendents.

Yes, Abram would be the father of a multitude of nations, and kings would come through him. But most importantly we find that kings would come through both Sarai and Abram. The implication is not only of coming kings, but also of a particular coming king—the King of kings. This King would be the one who dies for his subjects so that they may live. This King would be Jesus Christ. The first verse of the gospel of Matthew begins with "the record of the genealogy of Jesus the Messiah, the son of David, the son of Abraham." Jesus is the promised seed, the promised King who would bring blessings to all tribes, tongues,

---

[100]Hartley 171.

and nations. Therefore, Abram's descendants would be both physical and spiritual descendants.

The Lord would then give both Abram and Sarai a sign of the purposeful nature of his covenant with Abram. He would change first Abram's name, then Sarai's. In Genesis 17:5 God said, "No longer shall your name be called Abram, but your name shall be Abraham; for I will make you the father of a multitude of nations."

In Abraham's culture a name had power.[101] When a name was changed it was usually done to reflect a change in one's character or destiny.[102] For Abram, it was probably both, but more so to reflect the change of destiny for Abraham.

The name Abram means "exalted father." The name Abraham means "father of a multitude." One name looks to the past, the other looks to the future. One reflects the old, which has passed away; the other reflects the new.

God would not only reflect the change of character and destiny for Abraham, but he would do the same for Sarai as well. "Then God said to Abraham, 'As for Sarai your wife, you shall not call her name Sarai, but Sarah shall be her name." Sarai and Sarah have the same meaning in Hebrew, "princess." The name change for Sarah was to reflect the reality of her having children who would be kings over nations.

God's purpose in changing their names was so that every time Abraham and Sarah said their new names it would remind them that the covenant they entered into with the Lord was a purposeful covenant of hope and a destiny. By changing their names, God gave Abraham and Sarah a permanent sign of his purpose for their lives—to be the instruments that brought salvation to the world, to fulfill God's divine plan of redemption.

As the Lord expanded his covenant with Abram he in essence declared to Abram, "I have a plan and a purpose: to bring salvation to the world. I will use you to bring that plan about. I

---

[101]Walton and Matthews 44.
[102]Hartley 171.

will give your life purpose. I will give your life hope. I will give your life destiny. I will be your God and you will be my child. I will use you to introduce me to other people so that I can have a relationship with them as well."

The same is true for the Christian who enters a relationship with the Lord through faith in Jesus Christ. When we enter into a covenantal relationship with the Lord, we are given a new character and a new destiny. The apostle Paul said it like this: "If anyone is in Christ, he is a new creation; the old is gone, the new has come!" (2 Corinthians 5:17 NIV). When you are given the new name "Christian" you can be assured that God has a plan for your life. You can be assured that the Lord wants to use you to tell others about a personal relationship with him. When you are given the name "Christian" you can forget the past because the Lord has given you purpose, hope, and a destiny. You can be assured that your life has purpose and meaning.

While I was studying at Criswell College, I had many opportunities to work with international students. Many of those students were from Korea, and a lot of them were named Paul or Timothy. I later learned that these were not their birth names but their Christian names, names they received when they came to Christ—new names to reflect their purpose, their hope, and their destiny.

The purposeful nature of the covenant is comforting for those who have a relationship with the Lord. Many people spend their lives looking for their purpose, meaning, hope, and destiny, but they fail to find it because they fail to find the Lord. One person has said, "Living without God's plan for our life is like sewing with a needle without thread, or writing one's biography with a pen empty of ink."[103] But that is not the case for the Christian. God's purpose gives us the "Why" of life so that when we face life we can know the "How" of life.[104] The final

---

[103]Green 220.
[104]Green 220.

observation reveals that this covenant of comfort is found in the permanent nature of the covenant.

The Permanent Nature of the Covenant

The Lord declared the permanent nature of the covenant in Genesis 17:7–8. "I will establish my covenant between me and you and your descendants after you throughout their generations for an everlasting covenant, to be God to you and to your descendants after you. I will give to you and your descendants after you, the land of your sojournings, all the land of Canaan, for an everlasting possession; and I will be their God."

Twice in these two verses the Lord referred to his covenant as an everlasting covenant. At the heart of this great proclamation of the permanent nature of the covenant is the fact that the Lord said to Abraham, "I will be God to you and to your descendants after you" and "I will be their God." Just as the Lord committed himself to Abraham and his descendants in time, he also committed himself to Abraham and his descendants in eternity.

When God's people enter into a covenantal relationship with the Lord through faith in Christ, the Lord becomes our God and we become his people, not only in this life, but also in the life to come. God binds himself to his people for eternity. This is the great security that we have as believers, that the Lord will always be our God and we will always be his people.

In 1937 the construction of the Golden Gate Bridge was completed at a cost of seventy-seven million dollars. The bridge was constructed in two stages that contrasted one another. The first stage went rather slowly. During the first stage some twenty-three men fell to their death working on the bridge. The work on the first stage stopped because the construction workers were paralyzed by fear. Then someone came up with the idea of putting a safety net under the workers for their protection. The net's cost was around a hundred thousand dollars. It was the largest net built and hung. When the second phase of construction began, ten men fell to safety because of the net. The work was done some twenty-five percent faster on account of the net. What made the difference? The comfort that came from the security of the net!

Similarly, the permanent nature of the covenant brings comfort to those who have a covenantal relationship with the Lord. It comforts us to know that though we struggle with sin and strive to overcome it, at times falling short, the Lord will always be our God and we will always be his people. The permanent nature comforts because it guarantees us that we will truly overcome in the end. Nothing can separate us from the love of God that is in Christ.

The eternal security of the believer is just as important a doctrine as the doctrine of justification by faith. Without its permanent nature of everlasting life, the gospel would really not be good news at all. God's people would have no grounds for comfort. But thanks be to God, we have comfort in this life and in the life to come. We can be confident of the permanent nature of the covenant because the one who made the covenant is El-Shaddai, God Almighty, who is all-sufficient and all-powerful. The second aspect of the covenant is that it is a covenant of consecration.

A Covenant of Consecration

As stated earlier, God's covenantal relationship with man is based solely on God's goodness. God did not decide that we deserved to have a covenant relationship—that would be inconsistent with God's righteousness and justice. On account of God's righteousness and justice we deserve to be the object of God's wrath. But because of God's goodness, he bestows grace to the undeserving by extending a means of entering into a relationship with him.

Although God's covenant relationship with man is by grace, man still has his part to do. This does not mean that God's covenant of grace is conditional; instead, it means that those who have truly experienced God's covenant of grace should respond biblically. Christians are "not saved by good works, but saved for good works." Man's good deeds are the result of regeneration by experiencing the grace of God.

With all this said, we now come to the part of the covenant that reveals Abraham's obligations to the covenant. In a broad sense Abraham's covenant obligations are declared in Genesis 17:1 when the Lord says to Abraham, "I am God Almighty, walk before me, and be blameless." A good paraphrase of this declaration may go something like this: "Abraham, I, the Lord, have saved you by grace. I have committed myself to you, and all I ask of you is that you live a life of obedience to me. This would show your love and devotion to me." So you can see from this phrase that Abraham, as well as all who enter into a covenant relationship with the Lord, are obligated to love the Lord by living out God's Word.

One way that Abraham and his descendants could truly walk before the Lord and be whole is spelled out in verses 9 through 14. In these verses God gives a sign of the covenant, which he made with Abraham and his descendants. "God said further to Abraham, 'Now as for you, you shall keep my covenant, you and your descendants after you throughout their generations" (Genesis 17:9). Abraham and his descendants had a responsibility within the covenant, one of obedience. And one such form of obedience was about to be given with a physical sign.

The Physical Sign of the Covenant

Circumcision was the physical act and symbol God gave to Abraham and his descendants. "This is my covenant, which you shall keep, between me and you and your descendants after you: every male among you shall be circumcised" (Genesis 17:10).

Circumcision, the removal of the foreskin, was widely practiced in the Near East.[105] The oldest evidence of the practice of circumcision dates back to Egypt about 2300 BC. Though it was widely practiced in the Near East, the reasons for its practice varied. In Egypt, it was a way to mark slaves.[106] In other Near Eastern regions, it was used as a rite of passage from childhood to manhood or when males married.

Yet God would take something so common and give it special significance for his people.[107] For Abraham and his descendants it would not be a rite of passage from childhood to manhood. This is clearly stated in the Lord's directions to Abraham in verse 12, "and every male among you who is eight days old shall be circumcised throughout your generations." For the generation to come, it would be a ritual done at the age of eight days as an act of obedience on the part of a baby boy's parents. The sign of circumcision would be a mark of the covenant relationship between God and his people.[108] Yet the physical sign of the covenant held a spiritual significance for Abraham and his descendants.

The Spiritual Significance of the Sign

Though physical in nature, circumcision had spiritual significance. One word could describe the spiritual significance: consecration. We must differentiate three aspects of the consecration. First, circumcision was by no means a sacrament that brought salvation. The outward ritual means nothing if it does not convey an inward reality of the heart. Several passages

---

[105]Kinder 130.

[106]"Circumcision," *Microsoft Encarta 98 Encyclopedia,* CD-ROM (Microsoft Corporation, 1997).

[107]Walton and Matthews 44.

[108]Kinder 130.

within the Old Testament declare this truth. Two such passages are found in the book of Deuteronomy. In Deuteronomy 10:16 it says, "So circumcise your heart, and stiffen your neck no longer." And in Deuteronomy 30:6 it says, "Moreover the Lord your God will circumcise your heart and the heart of your descendants, to love the Lord your God with all your heart and with all your soul, so that you may live." Unfortunately, generations that followed Abraham would see circumcision as a means of salvation, rather than as a sign of a heart that has been transformed. However, circumcision was to be an outward sign of an inward reality, one that revealed a heart circumcised by the grace of God.

Second, the spiritual significance of consecration is that of community. The sign of the covenant symbolized that a person had been set apart or consecrated into the community of God's people. With this came a sense of belonging. It was a sign that the person fit in with God's community of peculiar people, a people who witnessed to the rest of the world the grace of God. Not only did it mean that the person was set apart for the community of God's people, but it also meant that the person was set apart to God.

It is significant to note from the text that non-Hebrews, that is, Gentiles, were welcomed into the covenant community, and they still had to identify with the covenant community through means of circumcision. We see this truth communicated in verses 12 and 13 when the Lord commands the servants and foreigners in Abraham's household also to be circumcised. The plan of God's redemption was and is open to all tribes, tongues, and nations. A spiritual significance of circumcision is found in its symbolic nature, as a sign that God has set a people apart for the purpose of being a community of people who belong to him.

A third aspect of consecration was that of being set apart for the purpose of holiness. The people of God are to be different than the people of the world. They are to be holy, just as the Lord who called them is holy. They are to avoid the pagan rituals and lifestyles of the people around them. Circumcision was a sign of this consecration. It was a sign of being set apart for holy purposes. The cutting away of the flesh symbolized the death to self and sin. It symbolized that cutting away of human effort. It symbolized the cutting away of the old self and the coming of the new self. It was a sign that if the inward reality had really occurred, a death to self and to sin would take place in the life of the person who has a covenant relationship with the Lord.

So you can see the spiritual significance of the sign for the people of God under the Old Covenant. But one may ask what significance does it have for those who are in a covenant relationship with the Lord under the New Covenant? Physical circumcision has no significance to the believer under the New Covenant. What really matters under the New Covenant is spiritual circumcision, a circumcision that is done not by a literal knife, but by the sanctifying work of the Holy Spirit. The sign of this inward reality is no longer physical circumcision. Under the New Covenant, the outward symbol of an inner reality is baptism.

Baptism is the initiation into the New Covenant. In the same manner as circumcision, baptism has no saving merit. Baptism is to be an outward sign of changed spiritual reality. But just as circumcision became an empty ritual for many under the Old Covenant, today baptism has also become a meaningless ritual for many. Sadly, countless people who have been baptized in the name of Jesus will not spend eternity with him because the outward ritual was not predicated by the spiritual regeneration of the heart.

Furthermore, baptism symbolizes that one has died to self and sin and now lives in newness of life in Jesus Christ. When people are baptized, they are submerged under the water as a symbol of death with Christ. Then they are brought up out of the water as a symbol of newness of life in Christ. The reality of a new life in Christ enables God's people to live holy and righteous lives. It is the new heart that comes from our relationship with the Lord that enables God's people to love him with all their heart, with all their soul, and with all their strength.

The symbol of baptism is also a sign that we are members of the body of Christ, that we are a part of a community of grace, that we are to be committed to the community of faith, and most importantly that we are to be committed to Jesus Christ, the head of the community. Baptism is a sign that we belong to a peculiar people and that we should be different from the people outside the community.

Many have heard the name Matthew Henry, a great theologian of old. In fact, I would not be surprised if you have his Bible commentaries on your shelves. But have you ever heard the name Philip Henry? Philip Henry was the father of Matthew Henry. Philip Henry had a great influence on his son. He penned some words for his children, which would become their baptismal statement. This declaration proclaims the truth about the covenant between God and man being a covenant of consecration.

> I take God to be my chief end and highest good.
> I take God the Son to be my prince and Savior.
> I take God the Holy Spirit to be my sanctifier, teacher, guide, and comfort.
> I take the Word of God to be my rule in all my actions and the people of God to be my people under all conditions.
> I do hereby dedicate and devote to the Lord all that I am, all that I have, and all I can do.
> And I do this deliberately, freely, and forever.[109]

At the heart of this statement is the reality that a covenant of God is one of consecration, set apart for holy and glorifying purposes, set apart to be a peculiar people, the people of God. We are a people controlled by the Spirit of God, a people who live a supernatural life, by faith, instead of a natural life, by carnal instinct. A third aspect of the covenant that is revealed in this passage of Genesis 17 is that of challenge. That is, God's covenant is a covenant of challenge.

---

[109]Swindoll 45.

A Covenant of Challenge

This aspect is revealed in Abraham's response to the Lord after he tells him that his wife Sarai, whose name is now Sarah, is going to have a child. God promised a child who would come through Abraham and his wife Sarah. After the Lord told Abraham that Sarah would give birth to a son, and that from her will come nations and kings, Abraham responded almost as he did back in Genesis 17:3 when, "Abraham fell on his face." In verse 3 Abraham responded in reverence, respect, and awe at the appearing of the Lord, but that is not the case in verse 17 where we are told that after Abraham heard the news of his aged Sarah having a child "Abraham fell on his face and laughed." In Abraham's response we see that the covenantal relationship with the Lord is one of challenge. When we enter into covenantal relationship with the Lord, he challenges us in our daily walk, just as he did with Abraham. The Lord will first challenge the limitations of Abraham's faith.

A Challenge to Abraham's Limitations

Some believe that Abraham's laugh was a laugh of doubt, that is, they think that Abraham doubted God's ability to fulfill is promise, but that is not the case. Abraham laughed because his own faith put limits on God. God wanted to challenge Abraham's limitations of faith by pushing him beyond. The Lord did this when he declared that Sarah would be the one to have the promised son.[110]

Abraham is a man of great faith. Though he had his share of mess-ups along the way, he has matured in his faith despite his mistakes. But Abraham still had room for maturity, as do all believers on this side of heaven, and it is here in his response that we see the limitations of his faith.[111] Genesis 17:17 tells us that

---

[110]Sailhamer 159.
[111]Sailhamer 159.

"Abraham fell on his face and laughed, and said in his heart 'Will a child be born to a man one hundred years old? And will Sarah, who is ninety years old, bear a child?" Abraham believed that God was going to bring about his promise, but he felt that by promising the child through Sarah, God had set himself up for failure. Here is a man who put limits on the omnipotence of God. Abraham's faith was limited because of his human comprehension of the situation.

I can just hear Abraham saying, "Lord, that sure is ambitious, but you are setting yourself up for failure. I mean Lord I am hundred, Sarah is ninety years old. Come on, Lord!" God would not only challenge Abraham's limitations of faith, but he would also challenge Abraham's comprehension of the situation.

A Challenge to Abraham's Comprehension

The limitations of Abraham's faith influenced his comprehension of the situation. Therefore, Abraham actually proposed an idea to God, an idea that he thought would surely help the Lord fulfill his promise. Look at verse 18: "And Abraham said to God, 'Oh that Ishmael might live before you!" This request was out of concern for Ishmael, but it also revealed a merely human comprehension of how God could fulfill his promise.

In Abraham's limited faith he believed that it only made sense that God fulfill his promise through Ishmael. Humanly speaking, it was truly impossible for Abraham and Sarah to have a child. So Abraham gave the Lord a sure-fire plan that would work, but the Lord had different plans. The Lord's response to this request challenged Abraham's comprehension. "But God said, 'No, but Sarah your wife will bear you a son, and you shall call his name Isaac; and I will establish my covenant with him for an everlasting covenant for his descendants after him." God rejected Abraham's plan, and again he reaffirmed that Sarah would give birth to the promised child.

This time the Lord declared that the child would be a son, and that his name would be Isaac, which means "to laugh." Isaac's name would be a constant reminder to Abraham of his limited faith and of God's infinite power. It would remind him that what is impossible by man's standards is truly possible by God's. Every time Abraham and Sarah would call out "Isaac," it would remind them that God's ways and thoughts are higher than man's. The Lord is able to do far more than we ever ask or think.

God's people, those in a covenantal relationship with him, need to remember that the Lord is in the business of pushing us beyond our limits when it comes to the area of faith. One of my criticisms of the extreme charismatic movement is that it seems they live only for the spectacular. Everything they do is or has to be a miracle. Though I criticize them for such extremism, I must also commend them for at least believing beyond their limits. I commend them for letting God push them beyond the limits of their faith. Too many times within the non-charismatic churches, including my own Baptist denomination, we don't let the Lord push us beyond our limits. We talk about the Lord being omnipotent, but we don't let his omnipotence stretch and challenge the limitations of our faith or our comprehension. Too many times we offer up Ishmael as an answer, when God wants to give us an Isaac.

A Challenge to Abraham's Patience

Abraham faced another challenge in his covenantal relationship with the Lord, that of patience. The Lord told Abraham in verse 20 that Ishmael would be taken care of and blessed, but that the covenant would be made with Isaac. In reaffirming the promise of Isaac, we see the Lord challenge Abraham's patience. "But my covenant I will establish with Isaac, whom Sarah will bear to you at this season next year" (Genesis 17:21). It would be yet another year until the promise of a child was fulfilled!

The Lord would fulfill his promise to Abraham some twenty-five years after he gave the promise to Abraham. For thirteen of those years the Lord was silent as Ishmael grew up. But now Abraham would have to wait one more year, a sure test of his patience and endurance. And Abraham would accept the challenge and continue to trust the Lord even though it pushed him beyond his limits and his comprehension.[112]

A Covenant of Compliance

Abraham's final response to the Lord's revelation is uncovered in verse 23. "Then Abraham took Ishmael his son, and all the servants who were born in his house and all who were bought with his money, every male among the men of Abraham's household, and circumcised the flesh of their foreskin in the very same day, as God had said to him."

In this response we see Abraham's obedience to the obligation to the covenant of grace, thus making the covenant of the Lord a covenant of compliance. Here we see Abraham obeying the command that the Lord gave him back in verse 9. Abraham's response also takes the reader back to the very first verse in Genesis 17 when the Lord commanded Abraham to "walk before [God], and be blameless." Abraham's response revealed that he was a faithful partner in the covenant relationship with the Lord.

Yes, the covenant was one of grace, but an appropriate response to the covenant of grace to those who receive it is that of obedience and compliance to the Lord, that is, the outworking of the experience of grace. One person has rightly said, "We signify our covenant relationship with the Lord through

[112]Hartley 175.

obedience."[113] I came across an old chorus that illustrates this point well.

> After all he's done for me,
> After all he's done for me,
> How can I do less than give him my best,
> And live for him completely,
> After all he's done for me.[114]

God's covenant with man is a covenant of grace, which brings comfort, consecration, and challenge, and one that deserves compliance. After all that God has done for his children, the least we can do is show our love for him by being obedient.

---

[113]John H. Walton, *Genesis: The NIV Application Commentary* (Grand Rapids: Zondervon, 2001) 469.
[114]Walton 469.

CHAPTER VIII:

IS ANYTHING TOO DIFFICULT FOR THE LORD?

Genesis 18:1–15

Introduction

Many times in our study of the life of Abraham we have noticed encounters between the Lord and Abraham. The voice of the Lord called Abraham to leave his familiar surroundings and go to the Land of Promise. The voice of the Lord, heard through Pharaoh, rebuked Abraham for leaving the Land of Promise and going to Egypt. The voice of the Lord told Abraham, after he separated from his nephew Lot, to look up and see the land that he was giving to Abraham's descendants. The voice of the Lord, heard through Melchizedek, reminded Abraham of his source of victory and blessing. And through the voice of the Lord in a vision, the Lord cut his covenant with Abraham in Genesis 15.

In all of the Lord's encounters with Abraham, three encounters had to do with the appearing of the Lord before Abraham. The first time that the Lord appeared to Abraham is found in Genesis 12:7. There we read, "The Lord appeared to Abram and said, 'To your descendants I will give this land.' " The next time the Lord appeared to Abraham is in Genesis 17.

There we are told in the very first verse, "Now when Abram was ninety-nine years old, the Lord appeared to Abram." The appearing of the Lord in Genesis 12 and 17 precedes the voice of the Lord. Most of the encounters have been audible and somewhat physical through means of visions. But two of those encounters are described in an actual manner of God's appearing. We can only speculate on how the Lord appeared, but the evidence given in Genesis 17:22 clearly reveals that at least one of these appearances of the Lord was visual. "When he had finished talking with him, God went up from Abraham."

In Genesis 18 we are once again confronted with the reality of the advent of the Lord to Abraham. That is, the Lord, after going up from Abraham in Genesis 17:22, will now once again appear to Abraham. "Now the Lord appeared to him by the oaks of Mamre" (Genesis 18:1). The text does not name the one to whom the Lord appeared, but we know that the antecedent to the personal pronoun "him" in verse 1 is none other than Abraham, last mentioned in Genesis 17.

The fact that the author uses a personal pronoun for Abraham instead of his proper name gives us an indication that this chapter is connected to the previous chapter where the Lord appeared to Abraham to reaffirm and expand his covenant with him. In Genesis 18 the Lord's appearing deals with the covenant with Abraham, but God will now expand upon it. This time he will reaffirm the promise of the child through Sarah, who, if not already aware of the promise, will hear of it from the Lord himself.

The narrative found in Genesis 18:1–15 is connected with the concept of covenant. One could say that what is revealed in these verses is the natural outworking of the covenant relationship. Two things really stick out in this narrative: intimate fellowship (Genesis18:1–8) and imminent fulfillment (Genesis 18:9–15). Both of these observations are centered on the Lord. The intimate fellowship reveals the close relationship between the Lord and those who are in a covenant relationship with him. The imminent fulfillment reveals the extraordinary ability of the

Lord to fulfill his covenant promises to his people. Take a minute to read the text and become familiar with these verses now. Notice in this first portion of the narrative the relationship between the Lord and Abraham.

> Now the LORD appeared to him by the oaks of Mamre, while he was sitting at the tent door in the heat of the day. When he lifted up his eyes and looked, behold, three men were standing opposite him; and when he saw them, he ran from the tent door to meet them and bowed himself to the earth, and said, "My Lord, if now I have found favor in Your sight, please do not pass Your servant by. Please let a little water be brought and wash your feet, and rest yourselves under the tree; and I will bring a piece of bread, that you may refresh yourselves; after that you may go on, since you have visited your servant." And they said, "So do, as you have said." So Abraham hurried into the tent to Sarah, and said, "Quickly, prepare three measures of fine flour, knead it and make bread cakes." Abraham also ran to the herd, and took a tender and choice calf and gave it to the servant, and he hurried to prepare it. He took curds and milk and the calf which he had prepared, and placed it before them; and he was standing by them under the tree as they ate. (Genesis 18:1–8)

Here, in the remaining portion of this narrative, observe the focus on God's ultimate fulfillment.

> Then they said to him, "Where is Sarah your wife?" And he said, "There, in the tent." He said, "I will surely return to you at this time next year; and behold, Sarah your wife will have a son." And Sarah was listening at the tent door, which was

> behind him. Now Abraham and Sarah were old, advanced in age; Sarah was past childbearing. Sarah laughed to herself, saying, "After I have become old, shall I have pleasure, my lord being old also?" And the LORD said to Abraham, "Why did Sarah laugh, saying, 'Shall I indeed bear a child, when I am so old?' Is anything too difficult for the LORD? At the appointed time I will return to you, at this time next year, and Sarah will have a son." Sarah denied it however, saying, "I did not laugh"; for she was afraid. And He said, "No, but you did laugh." (Genesis 18:9–15)

The intimate fellowship and the imminent fulfillment that is revealed in these fifteen verses are closely connected. Those who are in fellowship with the Lord can be sure that God will fulfill his promises. There is one rhetorical question in this passage that underscores this reality, "Is anything too difficult for the Lord?" (v. 14). The answer is obvious.

In observing this advent of the Lord we will examine the intimate fellowship as revealed in verses 1 through 8; and then we will observe the imminent fulfillment as revealed in verses 9 through 15. Then, after we understand what is taking place in this passage, we'll explore the immediate reality this passage bears on us today. Therefore, let us first look at the intimate fellowship declared at the advent of the Lord.

The Intimate Fellowship

The Intimate Revelation of the Relationship (vv. 1–2)

"Now the Lord appeared to him at the oaks of Mamre, while he was sitting at the tent of the door in the heat of the day." The tents that Abraham lived in were most likely made out of goatskin and were designed to hold the heat in by night and to let the cool breeze of the day blow through as the tent gave shade to the occupants by day.[115] It was the hottest part of the day so Abraham was sitting in the shade enjoying the cool breeze that would blow through his tent.

The author of the narrative reveals to us that it is the Lord who appeared to Abraham in verse 1. This declaration is for the reader so we know that what is taking place in these verses is none other than a divine advent of the Lord.

Unlike the previous appearances of the Lord to Abraham, this one tells us how the Lord manifested himself to Abraham in verse 2. "When he lifted up his eyes and looked, behold, three men were standing opposite him." The Lord appeared to Abraham in human form.

Some say that the three men in this passage represent the Trinity, but the Scriptures reveal otherwise. Genesis 19:1 tells us that two of the men were angels, so the three men in this passage are the Lord and two angels. (Theologians call this a theophany.)

The Intimate Response to the Relationship (vv. 3–8)

Whether Abraham knew from the start that the Lord was appearing to him is debatable. Some argue that he knew it was the Lord himself because of Abraham's hospitable response. But such hospitality was extended customarily to guests in the Near East. Others argue that Abraham knew the Lord was present because he addresses one of the men as "my Lord" in verse 3. The Hebrew word for Lord here is "Adoni." This word is used often to refer to God as the Lord. At the same time this word is also used to refer to someone who is in a position of authority. Whether Abraham knew whom he was speaking to is open for discussion. However, one thing is certain: at some point during

---

[115]Walton and Matthews 44.

the encounter with the three men, Abraham understood that he was speaking with the Lord.

At a minimum, Abraham believed that these men were from the Lord, if he did not understand that one of them actually was the Lord. I base this on Abraham's request in verse 3, "My Lord, if now I have found favor in your sight, please do not pass your servant by." The statement of favor as well as being a servant indicates that Abraham had some understanding of the divine nature of this visitation.

Though Abraham was showing hospitality common of Near Eastern tradition, the manner in which he responded suggests that he understood the divine nature of the situation. After Abraham welcomed his guests and communicated his desires to serve them, we are told in verse 6, "So Abraham hurried into the tent to Sarah, and said, 'Quickly, prepare three measures of fine flour, knead it and make bread cakes.' Abraham also ran to the herd and took a tender and choice calf and gave it to the servant, and he hurried to prepare it. He took curds and milk and the calf which he prepared, and placed it before them; and he was standing by them under the tree as they ate." Notice the actions in these verses, "hurried into the tent," "quickly prepare," "ran to the herd," and "hurried to prepare it." Abraham's swiftness indicates he had some knowledge that this visitation was of a divine nature.

The meal that took place in these verses was significant to the covenant that the Lord had made with Abraham. It was common practice, as revealed in both the non-biblical and biblical record, of eating a meal after cutting a covenant or treaty.[116] It was important that the two parties who entered into a covenant eat a meal together to symbolize the peaceful agreement that was just entered into.[117]

In Exodus 24 we see God making a covenant with the people of Israel on Mt. Sinai. After the covenant was made, the

---

[116]Ross 342.
[117]Ross 342.

people of the covenant ate and drank in peace before the Lord. In the Levitical code you find the peace offering. The intention of this offering was to signify that the people had a peaceful relationship with the Lord. In the book of Judges, Gideon has a visitation from the Lord, the Lord rains down fire upon Gideon's sacrifice, and Gideon names the altar "Jehovah Shalom" or "The Lord is peace." The point is that the communal meal and sacrifice signified that the people who participated in the meal had peace with God, which meant they had a close intimate fellowship with God.[118]

Another indication that this text reveals intimate fellowship with the Lord is that the three men were in Abraham's tent or home. Here lies the significance of the advent of the Lord to Abraham in this passage: the Lord is conveying that Abraham has peace with the Lord, that he is a friend of God, and that he has intimate fellowship with the Lord. And it is because Abraham has this intimate fellowship with the Lord that the Lord goes on to remind Abraham and to tell Sarah of the imminent fulfillment of his promise to Abraham.

The Imminent Fulfillment

The Imminent Realization

In verse 9 the Lord asked Abraham a question—most likely, a rhetorical one, "Where is Sarah your wife?" The fact that the stranger knew the name of Abraham's wife indicates divine attributes. If he knew her name, then he probably knew where she was. The question brings Sarah into the dialogue, albeit through her eavesdropping.

After the Lord brought Sarah into the conversation, he then gave the imminent realization of the fulfillment of his

---

[118]Ross 342.

promise in verse 10. " 'I will surely return to you at this time next year, and behold, Sarah your wife will have a son.' And Sarah his wife was listening at the tent door, which was behind him." The Lord became precise in his promise. He told Abraham, and Sarah indirectly, that they were going to have a son in a year, and Sarah would respond with an impossible reaction.

The Impossible Reaction

We see Sarah's impossible reaction in verses 11 and 12. "Now Abraham and Sarah were old, advanced in age; Sarah was past childbearing. Sarah laughed to herself, saying, 'After I have become old, shall I have pleasure, my lord being old also?" Just as Abraham laughed in Genesis 17, Sarah laughs. Abraham's laugh was not a total doubt of God's ability to fulfill his promise, just a laugh of human limitations on God's ability. But Sarah's laugh seems to be one of total doubt on God's ability to fulfill his promise.

Now, before we are too hard on Sarah, we must put ourselves in her shoes. We know from verse 11 that "Sarah was past childbearing." She had apparently already gone through the change of life. Humanly speaking she was unable to have children. Recognizing the impossible nature of the promise from a human standpoint, she wondered, "After I have become old, shall I have pleasure?" Sarah questioned her human ability to conceive without considering God's divine intervention.

The Incredible Recognized

Notice also that Sarah laughed to herself. No one could tell she was laughing—another indication that the visitor was divine. Only the Lord himself could have known that Sarah had laughed to herself. The Lord was able to see that Sarah didn't view the incredible nature of the promise, but the impossible nature of the promise from her human perspective.

The Lord pointed Sarah to recognize the incredible when he asked another rhetorical question in verse 14, "Is anything too difficult for the Lord?" The word translated "difficult" is the Hebrew word "pala." It can mean "to be wonderful," "to cause a wonderful thing to happen," or "to fulfill." In any case it seems to always have the idea of doing the surpassing or the extraordinary. The word speaks of the unusual, those things that are beyond human capabilities.[119]

The Lord declared that nothing is too wonderful for him; nothing is too extraordinary. What is beyond human capability is not beyond his ability. What is humanly impossible is divinely possible. The same God who made heaven and earth could fulfill this extraordinary promise. The same God who spoke and it came to be, who commanded and it stood firm, is the same God who can do that which surpasses human comprehension.

The Lord declared to Sarah his delight in performing all that seems impossible, all that seems too marvelous, all that seems too extraordinary, and yes, all that seems surpassing. After the Lord declared his delight by means of a rhetorical question, Sarah understood that this was no ordinary stranger, for "Sarah denied it however, saying, 'I did not laugh;' for she was afraid." Sarah's denial of her laughter and her fear is indication that she understood this to be from the Lord. She denied her doubt, but the Lord responded, "No, you did laugh."

And every time Sarah said or heard her soon-to-come son's name Isaac, she would be reminded of her doubt. She would be reminded that the Lord delights in doing the impossible, the extraordinary, the marvelous, and the surpassing. The appearing of the Lord to Abraham and Sarah communicated the intimate fellowship the Lord has with his people and God's ability to fulfill his promises to those who are in intimate fellowship with him.

Let me now drive this truth home by showing you the immediate reality of fellowship and fulfillment to those of us who

---

[119]Archer, Harris, and Waltke 723.

live under the New Covenant. In driving it home I want to take you to another advent or appearing of the Lord. This appearing of the Lord would come some two thousand years after the Lord's appearing to Abraham and Sarah, yet the nature of the appearing communicated the same things: fellowship, fulfillment, and future.

The Immediate Reality

Fulfillment

The Lord would appear to another woman, although, compared to Sarah, she was hardly a woman. Sarah was up there in age, but the woman that the Lord would appear to thousands of years later was a young girl, a virgin around thirteen years old. Sarah had been married for several years when the Lord appeared to her, but this young virgin girl was only engaged when the Lord appeared to her. Sarah was barren; this young girl had never had sexual relations, and she also wondered how God would accomplish a humanly impossible birth.

Yet, when the Lord appeared to this virgin girl and she asked, "How can this be?" (Luke 1:34), God would declare once again, this time in the form of a statement rather than a question, that nothing is too difficult for him. He would once again state his desire to do the extraordinary. But instead of a lady advanced in age, we have a mere child. God would have a young girl conceive of supernatural means. She would become pregnant apart from sexual relations with an earthly mate. She would conceive by means of the Holy Spirit and give birth to a son who would be fully God and fully man, born without sin, and she would name him Jesus because he would bring salvation to a dying world.

Of course you know—the young virgin's name was Mary. And after the Lord declared to her his plans for her he said, "For nothing will be impossible with God" (Luke 1:37). Instead of posing a rhetorical question to Mary, the Lord gave the obvious answer to the question.

The son of Mary would be the ultimate fulfillment of God's promise to Abraham. He would be the great King who would descend from Abraham and bring the blessing of salvation for both Jews and Gentiles alike. Not only did this advent of the Lord bring about fulfillment, but it also brought about fellowship.

Fellowship

Just as the advent of the Lord to Abraham communicated intimate fellowship and peace with God, the advent of the Lord some two thousand years later made possible the intimate fellowship and peace with the Lord.

Jesus Christ, the one born of Mary would be born without sin and live a sinless life. He would give his life as a ransom for many on the cross of Calvary. Just before his death the Lord had his disciples in the upper room as they observed the Passover feast. The Lord lifted up the bread and said, "This is My body which is given for you; do this in remembrance of Me" (Luke 22:19). He then lifted up the wine and (paraphrased) said, "This is my blood, shed for the remission of sins, drink in remembrance of me" (see Mark 14:22–25). This supper was to declare that the Lord was initiating the New Covenant and making it possible for man to truly have peace and intimate fellowship with the Lord.

Believers observe this truth every time we participate in the Lord's Supper. This ordinance reminds us that Christ's sacrificial death and our faith in that death enables us to experience God's forgiveness; it enables us have peace and intimate fellowship with the Lord. It is the fulfillment and fellowship in Christ that also gives those who belong to Christ a future with him.

Future

Right now, God's people enjoy only partial fellowship with the Lord. We are longing for the day when we have full fellowship, the day when we have that great marriage supper with the Lord, and we can be sure of that day's arrival.

The same God who said, "Is anything too difficult for the Lord?" is the same God who will bring us to that great marriage supper. The same God who said, "For nothing will be impossible with God" is the same God who will get us to our final destination.

The great rhetorical question of the Scriptures is this: "Is anything too difficult for the Lord?" And the great answer that the Lord always gives is "No!" The God who created the heavens and the earth is the same God who can make a barren womb fruitful. The God who can make a barren womb fruitful is the same God who can make a virgin girl pregnant by means of an immaculate conception. The God who can bring about an immaculate conception is the same God who can raise his Son to life on the third day. The God who can raise his Son to life on the third day is the same God who can promise salvation to all who come to his Son by faith. The same God who can do all these extraordinary things in history can also do them in your life as well.

The question "Is anything too difficult for the Lord?" deserves a personal response from you. Are there any problems, troubles, or circumstances in your own life that are too difficult for God to handle?[120] Absolutely not!

Some people struggle with God's ability to save. They say to themselves, "I am beyond forgiveness. Surely God cannot forgive the things I have done." I am here to tell you that the Lord can forgive the vilest of sinners who come to Jesus Christ by faith.

---

[120]Boice 607.

Some people struggle with family issues, financial issues, and other problems in their life and it seems that the problems are too difficult for the Lord, but the reality is that "nothing is impossible with God." God can and will take care of his people who are in a covenant relationship with him.

CHAPTER IX:

THE GREAT PRESERVATIVE

Genesis 18:16–33

Introduction

Our Lord Jesus Christ, in his great Sermon on the Mount, spoke about the need for his people to be the great preservative in a dying and rotting world. Jesus taught this great truth using two metaphors, "You are the salt of the earth" and "You are the light of the world." Do these sound familiar?

Using these metaphors, the Lord Jesus impressed on God's people the need to be preservatives in a sin-saturated world. Salt is a preservative that maintains; light is a preservative that reveals. In a world where God's glory is blasphemed, sin is rampant, and the knowledge of God is becoming less and less, God's people are to be the great preservatives maintaining and revealing the glory of God, the holiness and righteousness of God, the salvation of God, and the knowledge of God.

The people of God, by their presence and practice, preserve these things. We act as salt that maintains God's righteousness and holiness. We act as light that reveals God's truth, salvation, and glory. This responsibility of being the great preservative of God's glory began early in human history, even before Abraham. God revealed this great truth to Abraham personally when he appeared to him in Genesis 18. It was only fitting that Abraham understood his responsibility as a great preserver since he would be the father of the nation of Israel, and more specifically, the father of the life of faith.

God declared the physical and spiritual responsibilities to Abraham and his descendants in Genesis 18:16–33. The responsibility of being the great preservative in a dying and decomposing world stems from the position of God's people. In verses 16 through 21, we see the position that preserves.

> Then the men rose up from there, and looked down toward Sodom; and Abraham was walking with them to send them off. The LORD said, "Shall I hide from Abraham what I am about to do, since Abraham will surely become a great and mighty nation, and in him all the nations of the earth will be blessed? For I have chosen him, so that he may command his children and his household after him to keep the way of the LORD by doing righteousness and justice, so that the LORD may bring upon Abraham what He has spoken about him." And the LORD said, "The outcry of Sodom and Gomorrah is indeed great, and their sin is exceedingly grave. I will go down now, and see if they have done entirely according to its outcry, which has come to Me; and if not, I will know." (Genesis 18:16–21)

The Position that Preserves

Verse 16 serves as a transition, a shift from blessing and favor to judgment and rejection, "Then the men rose up from there, and looked down toward Sodom; and Abraham was walking with them to send them off." We are reminded in this transition verse that God appeared to Abraham in human form. Three men appeared at the tent of Abraham. One of these men is believed to be the second person of the Trinity, the pre-incarnate Christ. The other two men are angels.

The men arise and look down toward Sodom. This sets the scene for what is going to take place, not only in the immediate verses of Genesis 18, but also in the impending verses of Genesis 19. But this is not the first time that the narrative sets the scene for what is going to take place with Sodom. The scene was set back in Genesis 13 when Abraham and his nephew Lot separated for the sake of peace. Abraham gave Lot the first choice of where to settle, and he chose the area near Sodom because it looked better. During that separation the author revealed that looks are deceiving. Sodom was not truly appealing because wickedness saturated the city.

We meet Sodom again in Genesis 14 when the four kings go up against the five. The king of Sodom was one of those five kings. Abraham would save the king of Sodom and his nephew Lot from the powerful four monarchs. Now in Genesis 18, once again, all eyes are on Sodom and on what God is going to do there. But first we get some background about how Abraham fits into the scheme of things and how he is to be a participant of sorts. In verses 17 through 19 the Lord talked with the other two men. This dialogue set the background, as the Lord revealed once again the promised position of Abraham.

The Promised Position

"The Lord said, 'Shall I hide from Abraham what I am about to do?' " The Lord is referring to what is about to take place in Sodom; all that follows encompasses the reason he gives for letting Abraham in on his plan. "Shall I hide from Abraham what I am about do, since Abraham will surely become a great nation, and in him all the nations of the earth will be blessed?" This promise of Abraham becoming a great nation, and his being a blessing to all nations was revealed to Abraham back in Genesis

12. Time and again God reminds Abraham of this great promise of position.

It is significant that we understand this promise of position in light of what is going to happen. Through our study we know that ultimately God blessed all the nations through Abraham by having the Savior of the world come from his seed. But this promised position also speaks of Abraham's responsibility of being a blessing bearer to the rest of the world. One of the ways that Abraham would be a blessing to all the world is that he would be a great preservative of the truth of God, the salvation of God, the knowledge of God, and so on. This promised position given by God to Abraham was also a privileged position.

The Privileged Position

The privileged position is revealed in the first part of verse 19 where it says, "For I have chosen him." There is a great deal of theology packed into that small phrase, a theology that we call divine election. It is in Abraham's divine election that we see his privileged position. In fact, it is in Abraham's privileged position that we find the cause of his promised position.

The Hebrew word "yada" is the word that we translate "chosen." It can also be translated "know." The verb speaks of selecting a person for the purpose of developing a close and intimate relationship with that person. The same word is used in Genesis 4:1 where it speaks of Adam knowing his wife in sexual relations; again the idea conveyed is intimacy. Because the Lord has chosen Abraham, he has blessed him with the promised position, which is based upon Abraham being a friend of and in a covenantal relationship with the Lord.

God's selecting Abraham is what we call divine election. Divine election is not based on anything within Abraham; that is why we call divine election unconditional. God's election is based upon his grace and goodness alone. Because the Lord decided before the foundation of the world to have a covenant relationship with Abraham, he found himself a recipient of God's promised position. With this wonderful and privileged position came not only the promised position, but also the purposeful position.

The Purposeful Position

The position that Abraham enjoyed on the basis of God's grace had a purpose, and that purpose was to be a great preserver of the knowledge of God from one generation to the next. What was the purpose of Abraham's privileged position? Verse 19 tells us, "For I have chosen him, so that he may command his children and his household after him to keep the way of the Lord by doing righteousness and justice, so that the Lord may bring upon Abraham what he has spoken about him."

Abraham and all who live a life of faith are a blessing to all nations by being propagators of the knowledge of God from one generation to the next. God's people have a position that preserves in that they must walk in the way of the Lord and they must teach their children and every generation after to walk in the way of the Lord.

Studies have revealed that there are no records of schools within the Jewish culture until the intertestamental period, that is, the era between the Old and New Testaments. The reason for the absence is found here in this verse. The education of the Hebrew nation took place within the family structure.[121] The spiritual and ethical heritage of the Jewish nation was passed down from one generation to the next through the family. This is consistent with what is called the Shema in Deuteronomy 6:4–9 where the Lord, through Moses, commands the people of Israel to love the Lord God with all their heart and to teach their children the commands of God.

---

[121]Waltke 269.

In fact, one can turn to the New Testament and find a wonderful illustration of the propagation of the knowledge of God from one generation to the next. The illustration is found in 2 Timothy where we are told that Timothy's mother and grandmother taught him the Scriptures. One of the main books of the Bible that Jews would use for the education of the next generation was the book of Proverbs where God's people learn about the fear of the Lord and how to live a righteous life.

The purposeful position brought about the responsibility of propagating the knowledge of God from one generation to the next through the family unit. Commanding future generations to "keep the way of the Lord" accomplished this. The phrase "the way of the Lord" is what one person calls a "technical metaphor." It speaks of "right living in community that leads to the right destiny do to one's relationship with the Lord."[122] Or another way to describe the "way of the Lord" is to let our whole course of life be lived out in conformity to our covenant obligations to the Lord. One of the ways that we live in conformity to our relationship with the Lord is by practicing righteousness and justice.

Focus on verse 19 again: "For I have chosen him so that he may command his children and his household after him to keep the way of the Lord by doing righteousness and justice." Walking in the way of the Lord by doing righteousness and justice serves as a preservative in an unrighteous and unjust world. To do righteousness means that God's people promote a social order that conforms to God's rule.[123] In other words, we act as salt and light by promoting a social order that conforms to the righteousness of God. Those who say that you cannot legislate morality are misguided. All law is morality. The question is, Which morals are you going to legislate? God's people serve as preservatives by promoting a social order that conforms to God's rule.

---

[122]Waltke 269.
[123]Waltke 269.

If righteousness promotes a social order that is in conformity with God's rule, then justice restores a community when those within the community do not live in conformity to God's rule. Justice can take the form of punishment for the oppressor and deliverance for the oppressed. Justice can work its way out in many areas of a society, but it has in mind the restoration of a community.[124] Abraham was to be a model of God's righteousness and justice by practicing it throughout his life. By doing so Abraham would be a preservative of the knowledge of God and all that comes with the knowledge of God, such as righteousness, justice, salvation, holiness, and so on. Through the family, Abraham was to make sure that from one generation to the next there was a constant preservative for God's cause.

Those who live a life of faith are in a position of being preservatives, that is, salt and light. One of the ways that we propagate our spiritual and ethical heritage is through the education of our family. We must teach the next generation that the "fear of the Lord is the beginning of wisdom" (Psalm 111:10). We must teach the next generation that God delights in his people promoting righteousness and justice in the way they live their lives. We must teach the next generation so that, even in our sin-saturated world, the glory of God and the knowledge of God are preserved.

Some of you may have heard of Saint Simeon the Stylite. He was a Christian who lived around AD 400. He lived in a monastery, until one day he decided to leave. After, Simeon took up residence on a platform atop a stone "stylite," the Greek word for pillar. He eventually made his home atop a sixty-foot high pillar. He did not descend from this abode during the last thirty years of his life. People would come from all over to hear Simeon preach from his pillar and, as a result, many unbelievers were converted to Christianity.

---

[124]Waltke 269.

One day, a young boy came across the story of Simeon in his reading. He was so mesmerized by the story that he decided to follow in Simeon's footsteps. So the young boy, whose name was Brian, went to the kitchen and got on top of a tall barstool. His mother heard something in the kitchen and went to find out what the ruckus was. When she arrived in the kitchen she found her son standing on the barstool. "Brian, get down from there," she cried, "You are going to get hurt!" In frustration, he got down from the barstool and whined, "You can't even become a saint in your own house."

How tragic it would be that God's people fail to create an atmosphere where their children cannot become saints, where their children do not become preservers of God's glory and knowledge in a godless world. God's people must teach their children to keep the way of the Lord by doing righteousness and justice. We must teach by telling and by example.

The life of faith puts us in a position that helps preserve the knowledge of God. One of the ways we preserve God's glory and knowledge is through teaching this generation and the next generation to walk in the way of the Lord. The first few verses of this section of Genesis 18 reveal that God's people serve as preservers for the Lord's cause through instruction, and the remaining verses show that God's people serve as preservers for the Lord's cause through intercession.

The Petition that Preserves

Verses 16 through 19 serve as the background for what is going to take place in subsequent verses. They reveal to us the reason the Lord brings Abraham into the situation that will take place in Sodom. So the Lord tells Abraham in verses 20 and 21, "The outcry of Sodom and Gomorrah is indeed great, and their sin is exceedingly grave. I will go down now, and see if they have done entirely according to this outcry, which has come to me; and if not, I will know." The situation that is about to take place in

Sodom and Gomorrah is based upon two things: the great outcry from and the grievous sin in Sodom and Gomorrah.

The Hebrew word translated "outcry" is often used elsewhere of those who are being illegitimately treated, oppressed by an oppressor. Whatever the cry is about, the Lord makes sure the judgment that will occur in Sodom and Gomorrah is based upon the grievous sin that is taking place in the city. The moral depravity of the city had become so great that the Lord would have to deal with it.

The Lord's description of the "outcry" and "sin" reveals that no sin goes unseen by God. Although without careful interpretation, the verses seem to suggest that the Lord does not possess that unlimited knowledge. For if he did, then why does he have to go down to confirm the "outcry" and the "sin"? We should not interpret these verses as showing God with limited knowledge of the situation. Instead, God's "investigation" of the sinful situation in Sodom reveals God's mercy. Yes, God is righteous and just and he must give sin and sinners what they deserve, but he is also a God of mercy who, by investigating, shows compassion to the objects of his impending judgment. Because of his holy and merciful character, the Lord by no means acts hastily in his judgment of sinners. Instead, he is long-suffering with them, not wanting any to perish, but desiring all to come to repentance.

What kind of outcry does the Lord hear from the cities of our nation? There have been times I have reflected upon the immensity of God and realized there is not a sin that God does not see. Not one evil act goes unnoticed by the Lord. He hears the cry of the child who is being abused by an alcoholic father. He hears the cry of the prostitute and the drug dealer. He hears the cries of sexual depravity. He hears the cries of all the grievous sins that are committed. And God in his righteousness and justice is totally justified to act quickly in passing judgment, but instead he shows mercy, giving people a chance to turn from their sins.

Not only do we see the mercy of God revealed in the investigation of the situation, but we also see the mercy of God revealed in Abraham's participation in the situation, which is to intercede for both the righteous and the unrighteous. Abraham would be a blessing to all the nations by being the great preservative. He would do this by propagating the way of the Lord from one generation to the next. He would also be a great preservative in a sin-saturated world through his petitions for the lost.

As the two men left, the Lord stayed behind with Abraham, and we are told in verse 22 that "Abraham was still standing before the Lord." The same verb "stand before" is used in the book of Jeremiah and refers to the prophet Jeremiah standing before the Lord and interceding for the people.[125] That is exactly what the Lord has Abraham doing in verse 22, interceding for the people, both righteous and unrighteous, in the sin-filled city of Sodom and Gomorrah. We see that God's people serve as light and salt by means of intercession for the lost and dying. The first thing we notice about the petition that preserves is the concern of the petition.

The Concern of the Petition

Before we go on, let's review this next passage of Scripture, Genesis 18:22–33.

> Then the men turned away from there and went toward Sodom, while Abraham was still standing before the LORD. Abraham came near and said, "Will You indeed sweep away the righteous with the wicked? Suppose there are fifty righteous within the city; will You indeed sweep it away and not spare the place for the sake of the fifty righteous who are in it? Far be it from You to do such a thing, to slay the righteous with the wicked,

---

[125]Victor P. Hamilton, *The Book of Genesis Chapters 18–50* (Grand Rapids: William B. Eerdmans Publishing Co., 1995) 23.

> so that the righteous and the wicked are treated alike. Far be it from You! Shall not the Judge of all the earth deal justly?" So the LORD said, "If I find in Sodom fifty righteous within the city, then I will spare the whole place on their account." And Abraham replied, "Now behold, I have ventured to speak to the Lord, although I am but dust and ashes. "Supposed the fifty righteous are lacking five, will You destroy the whole city because of five?" And He said, "I will not destroy it if I find forty-five there." He spoke to Him yet again and said, "Supposed forty are found there?" And He said, I will not do it on account of the forty." Then he said, "Oh may the Lord not be angry, and I shall speak; suppose thirty are found there?" And He said, "I will not do it if I find thirty there." And he said, "Now behold, I have ventured to speak to the Lord; suppose twenty are found there?" And He said, "I will not destroy it on account of the twenty." Then he said, "Oh may the Lord not be angry, and I shall speak only this once; suppose ten are found there?" And He said, "I will not destroy it on account of the ten." As soon as He had finished speaking to Abraham the LORD departed, and Abraham returned to his place.

As Abraham stands before the Lord, we see the concern of his petition. "Will you indeed sweep away the righteous with the wicked?" This question is sometimes understood in two conflicting ways. Some say that Abraham is questioning the righteousness of God. Others say that this statement is not a question of God's righteousness, but rather a statement of Abraham's faith in God's righteousness.

Those who hold to the former view say that Abraham is putting himself in God's position as Judge, but that is not the case. Abraham understands that the Lord is the Judge of all the earth, for he states this fact in a subsequent verse 25. Therefore, Abraham is not putting himself in the position of Judge by questioning God's righteousness. Instead, Abraham is stating his faith that God will always do right in every situation, especially when it comes to judgment.

This statement of faith in the form of a rhetorical question reveals that Abraham's petition grew out of a concern for the righteous. As God would make his way down to Sodom and pass judgment, Abraham was concerned about his nephew Lot and his family. Abraham's concern is fleshed out even more as he continued to plead for the righteous living in a wicked land. "Suppose there are fifty righteous within the city; will you indeed sweep it away and not spare the place for the sake of the fifty?" Abraham continued to plead with the Lord, asking God to spare the city for the sake of only ten righteous people. This shows us the concern Abraham had for the righteous. But just as important was Abraham's sorrow for the unrighteous.

When the Lord used Abraham to rescue the king of Sodom and his people (back in Genesis 14), Abraham came to personally know and care for the king of Sodom and many of the lost people in the land. Therefore he pleaded not only for the righteous, but also for the whole place, that the Lord would not destroy the sinful city as long as any of the great preservatives, the righteous, lived there. Just as God has compassion and love for both the righteous and the unrighteous, his people must demonstrate the same compassion. Though we can't fully understand God's plan of election and human responsibility, we know that God wants us to demonstrate love, compassion, and mercy through intercessory prayer for the lost.

I am reminded of how our Lord Jesus Christ mourned over Jerusalem (Matthew 23:37–39). The body of Christ must do the same. The concern of our petition must be for the righteous as well as for the unrighteous. We must be great preservatives by means of praying for the unrighteous, that they may come to repentance. We must pray that the Lord would convict them of their sin, that he would open their spiritual eyes, that he would reveal himself to them, that he would draw them to him, and that he would bind the hold that Satan has upon their lives.

Are you concerned about the downward spiral of our nation's morality? Then pray for God's grace to be poured out on the unrighteous. The unrighteous should be thankful for the prayers on behalf of this nation, as America might have been swept away long ago had it not been for the righteous petitions of believers. But not just any prayer of a person living a life of faith preserves. The characteristics of the petition are vital; we must pray with humility and persistence and according to the nature of God.

The Characteristics of the Petition

Recorded here in Genesis 18 is the first intercessory prayer in the Bible. Abraham provides an exemplary model of the characteristics of all prayer.[126] You could say that Abraham gives us a prototype of intercessory prayer.[127]

The first characteristic we notice about Abraham's prayer is that it was done in humility. Abraham's humility is revealed in two ways. Abraham did not need to know the deep things of God in order to pray for the lost. He did not have to know about God's

[126]Morris 344.
[127]Morris 344.

ultimate purpose for the unrighteous or righteous before he prayed for them. He humbled himself before a sovereign God understanding that, no matter the outcome, God would act justly in the situation. Even if from Abraham's standpoint it looked as if God acted unjustly, he was confident that the Lord would do what was right. That is humility.

Another declaration of Abraham's humility before the Lord is found in his words to the Lord in verse 27, "Now behold, I have ventured to speak to the Lord, although I am but dust and ashes." Abraham understood that his position before the Lord was by God's grace and mercy, and nothing within him demanded that the Lord listen.[128]

The second characteristic of Abraham's prayer is that it was persistent. Abraham did not stop asking the Lord for an answer after he petitioned for the fifty righteous people within the city. Abraham petitioned persistently until he got to ten righteous people in the city and until the answer he received was loud and clear. The clarity of God's answer was undoubtedly that the Lord would act justly in this and in every situation.

The persistence that Abraham demonstrated here is familiar to those who have witnessed a business transaction in the Middle East. A lot of haggling takes place.[129] But we should not think that Abraham is trying to force God's hand so to speak. Instead we should see this as the Lord "drawing Abraham on" in his faith. Persistent prayer is a sign of faith. I encourage you to read the parable of the persistent widow in Luke 18 to further illustrate this truth.[130]

The third characteristic is that Abraham's prayer was grounded in the very nature of God. Abraham's petition is not based upon his own character, but upon God's. Abraham appeals to the Lord to answer on the basis of God's righteousness, mercy, and love. He appeals to God to answer on the basis of God's

---

[128]Boice 616.
[129]Walton and Matthews 45.
[130]Boice 616.

glory and honor. Like Abraham, when his people plead according to the nature of God, we glorify and honor him. Moses also exemplified this when he prayed for the Israelites (Exodus 32:11–14). The Lord was ready to destroy his people on account of their sin, but Moses interceded for them on the basis of God's glory and honor, and the Lord spared those facing judgment on the basis of Moses' intercession for them. Finally, what we notice about the petition that preserves is the confidence that the Lord will do what is right in every situation.

The Confidence of the Petition

After persisting in prayer with the Lord, verse 33 tells us that "as soon as he finished speaking with Abraham the Lord departed, and Abraham returned to his place." Abraham persisted in prayer with the Lord until he appealed even if only ten righteous people lived within the city. After the Lord responded to the request of ten, Abraham would no longer petition for the city of Sodom and the righteous in it. This is interesting when you realize that the only righteous people in the city numbered four: Lot, his wife, and their two daughters. Abraham stopped because he was confident that however the Lord answered his petition he would do so in righteousness and justice.

Now, as the story unfolds in Genesis 19 we will see how the Lord answered the prayer for the city of Sodom. Instead of sparing the city on account of the four righteous people, the Lord took Lot and his family out of Sodom and he rained down judgment upon the city. To some this may seem unjust, but we can be assured that the Lord was righteous and just in his dealings with Sodom. He did not pass judgment upon the city dwellers hastily, but instead he allowed Abraham to intercede on their behalf. God would bring righteous judgment upon Sodom and Gomorrah.

Some look at the judgment of Sodom and Gomorrah and wonder, "Why doesn't God overlook our sin?"[131] The answer is to bring glory to a perfect and holy God. His righteous acts of judgment contrast our imperfection, ultimately bringing glory to him. We may not always understand why or how God answers intercessory prayer, but we can be confident that he will answer in a way that is totally right, for the Lord is the standard of righteousness. The last thing we must observe about God's people being the great preservative is the presence that preserves.

The Presence that Preserves

The presence that preserves is found in the four righteous people the Lord would safeguard, Lot's family. When the Lord decided to bring judgment upon Sodom and Gomorrah, he told Lot and his family to go to the mountains. But Lot asked the Lord if he could go to the city of Zoar. The Lord granted his request and spared Zoar from judgment (Genesis 19:21). The very presence of the righteous preserves the knowledge of God, and God temporarily preserved the unrighteous from judgment. Some of you are in a situation that seems unbearable because of the ungodliness of it. Let this truth about Lot serve as an encouragement to you, that your very presence can make a difference in the life of the unrighteous.

In a recent Christian news documentary, I learned about a place in Ireland called the Bangor Abby. It was a monastery that was established in Ireland soon after St. Patrick died around AD 550. The man who brought leadership to the monastery was convicted of the need for the monks to have worship and prayer around the clock. In shifts, the monks would pray and worship the Lord. They prayed continually for the lost in the country and they matched their petition for the lost with a missionary zeal for the lost. Historians attribute the prayer from the monastery as the

---

[131]Boice 616.

greatest preservative from keeping Ireland and the surrounding countries from falling into deep darkness.

The church, the holy mountain of God that is high and lifted up to the heavens is the great preservative. We are in position that preserves, a position that must be passed down from one generation to the next. We must participate in the petition that preserves. We must realize that our presence preserves.

CHAPTER X:

THE SPIRITUAL DECLINE OF THE SPIRITUALLY INCLINED

Genesis 19:1–38

Introduction

Genesis 19 is an interesting chapter to say the least, for it encompasses several views. We can see the standpoints of a sinful world, of God answering the prayers of the righteous, and of God's people falling into a spiritual decline that has devastating consequences. And because of these different standpoints within the chapter there are several approaches that an expositor can take.

One could look at this chapter from the standpoint of God's judgment upon the sinful cities of Sodom and Gomorrah. The wickedness of Sodom is no surprise as we come to this nineteenth chapter. The book of Genesis starts pointing out the sinful condition of this city back in chapter 13. But God's patience has come to an end, and he now brings judgment upon a city and a people who have rejected the knowledge of God. Before you begin to think God unfair for his judgment upon this sinful city, let me just point out that when the Lord first revealed the sinful condition of Sodom, it was some twenty or more years before. The Lord does not act hastily in his judgment, but is patient, not wanting any to perish.

There is a great warning in Genesis 19 for all nations, especially for the United States. The hallmark of the grievous sin that consumed the cities of Sodom and Gomorrah was homosexuality. Such was the case when the two men (who were really two angels) showed up in the city; all the men of the city wanted to gang rape the two heavenly hosts. Because the moral condition of our own nation is not far behind Sodom and Gomorrah's, Americans should be concerned that we too will face the judgment of God. I have to agree with one commentator who said, "If God does not judge America, then the Lord will have to apologize to Sodom and Gomorrah."[132]

Genesis 19 also allows us to observe the close connection to Abraham's petition for both the righteous and the unrighteous, as we studied in Genesis 18. We will see the results of Abraham's standing in the gap for the righteous and unrighteous alike. Before the Lord rained down judgment upon the city, he rescued Abraham's nephew Lot and his family. We often look at the rescue of Lot as being on the basis of Lot's righteousness. And he was righteous, for Peter tells us in his second letter that "righteous" Lot was rescued from Sodom. But Genesis 19 reveals in two places that Lot was rescued for other reasons.

In verse 16 we read, "But he [Lot] hesitated. So the men seized his hand and the hand of his wife and the hands of his two daughters, for the compassion of the Lord was upon him; and they brought him out, and put him outside the city." As we will notice later, Lot hesitated to leave the city, but God would have compassion on him and rescue him anyway.

Another reason Lot was rescued is revealed in verse 29. "Thus it came about, when God destroyed the cities of the valley, that God remembered Abraham, and sent Lot out of the midst of the overthrow, when he overthrew the cities in which Lot lived." Abraham's petition for his nephew resulted in Lot's rescue. That

---

[132]Phillips 158.

is why it is important that we stand up for the righteous and unrighteous alike.

I have chosen to approach this multifaceted chapter from the standpoint of "righteous Lot," and his spiritual decline. Until now, our study has focused more on the life of Abraham and how God worked in his life. But it is beneficial for us to observe Lot's life and how he refused to let God work in his life. God's people, especially those who think that spiritual decline is beyond them, can learn from Lot's experience. Paul warns us of such pride in 1 Corinthians 10:12 when he says, "So, if you think you are standing firm, be careful that you don't fall." Paul warns us of the possibility of spiritual decline, and the greatest candidates for it are those who think it could never happen to them. This is precisely what happened to Lot. How did righteous Lot end up in a place like Sodom and Gomorrah? How could he stray so far from his great start? Lot's spiritual decline was gradual.

The Spiritual Decline Is Gradual

As we observe Lot, don't think for a moment that Lot's condition, as revealed in Genesis 19, happened suddenly. The spiritual decline was gradual, but continual. When we first met Lot back in Genesis 11, Abraham's father, Terah, took not only Abraham and his wife, but also Lot to the Land of Promise, Canaan. But Terah did not make it to Canaan, instead he settled in Haran. After Terah died, the Lord again called Abraham to go to the land of Canaan. Abraham obeyed and Lot went with him.

We can only speculate on why Lot decided to go with Abraham. It would be a reasonable supposition to believe that Lot went with his uncle on a voluntary basis and that his tagging along with his uncle was done out of an act of faith in the Lord as well. Whatever the case may be, Lot decided to venture with his uncle on this journey of faith. Unfortunately, Lot did not follow in his uncle's footsteps, but instead he made choices in his life that would bring him to the spiritual bankruptcy we read about in Genesis 19.

The first step of Lot's spiritual decline started many years before, back in Genesis 13 where Abraham and Lot separated for the sake of peace. After Abraham told Lot to choose his direction, "Lot lifted up his eyes and saw all the valley of the Jordan, that it was well watered everywhere—this was before the Lord destroyed Sodom and Gomorrah—like the garden of the Lord, like the land of Egypt as you go to Zoar" (Genesis 13:10). Lot looked, saw, and chose the valley of the Jordan on the basis of appearance alone. Yet, what seemed to be especially appealing was really not, for we are told several times that the men of Sodom were exceedingly wicked. As Abraham and Lot separated, we are told in Genesis 13:12 that Lot "moved his tents as far as Sodom."[133] Lot pitched his tents right outside the sinful city.

We find the second step in Lot's spiritual decline in Genesis 14. In this chapter the city of Sodom is attacked and the people living there are taken captive. Verse 12 shows us the decline of Lot, "They also took Lot, Abram's nephew, and his possessions and departed, for he was living in Sodom." In Genesis 13 Lot is living outside of Sodom; in Genesis 14 Lot is living in Sodom.

When we get to Genesis 19 we read, "Now the two angels came to Sodom in the evening as Lot was sitting in the gate of Sodom." Lot not only lives in Sodom at this point, but he is also now one of the leaders in the city. To be sitting at the gate of Sodom suggests that Lot was in a high-ranking position, for many important decisions and judgments were made there. For Lot to be sitting at the gate of a sinful city such as Sodom suggests that the inhabitants of Sodom accepted him. Though he was a righteous man, his spiritual decline kept him from being a

---

[133]Sailhamer 171.

champion of righteousness and justice in a sin-saturated city.[134] This reveals the gradual process of Lot's spiritual decline.

At the heart of this gradual process were Lot's sensual and sinful desires. The apostle John in his first epistle spoke about these sensual and sinful desires when he spoke about the lust of the flesh, the lust of the eyes, and the pride of life. These lusts, John warns, are of the world. The gradual process of spiritual decline takes place when God's people are led by sensual sinful desires instead of by the expectations of the Savior.

You begin to see the sensual aspect of Lot's demise when you compare Lot with Abraham. When they separated Abraham was willing to trust the Lord to lead him, whereas Lot was led by what he saw. Abraham lived in a tent, whereas Lot desired more than a tent and would eventually move into a house. Abraham was a pilgrim looking for the celestial city, whereas Lot was a citizen enjoying the benefits of the world.[135]

As God's people, we are by no means free from the temptations of the lust of the flesh, the lust of the eyes, and the pride of life, but we are free from being slaves to them. The gradual process of spiritual decline takes place when we begin to give into and be consumed with the sensual and sinful desires that belong to this world.

Throughout biblical history and in our own time, we find men of God falling into spiritual decline, a decline that was a gradual process. King David did not wake up one day and declare, "I think I am going to commit adultery today." David's decline was a gradual process of leaving sinful desires unchecked. With Lot also, his inability to deal with sin gradually led him to a moral earthquake. Today, we hear about preachers or other Christian leaders falling, and we need to understand that their decline didn't happen overnight. It was a gradual process, a process that came about from some moral fault lines within their lives.

---

[134]Phillips 159.
[135]Phillips 159.

Just recently an earthquake with a 7.6 magnitude shook central Mexico killing several people. This earthquake didn't just happen. There were things taking place beneath the ground's surface long before the earthquake erupted and destroyed lives. The spiritual decline of those who are spiritually inclined is similar; things are happening beneath the surface long before we see the moral earthquake take place. When God's people don't deal with underlying sin issues, they lead us to a spiritual decline. And when we don't deal with the spiritual decline, it brings destructive consequences.

The Spiritual Decline Is Destructive

As the story of Lot unfolds in Genesis 19, we begin to see the destructiveness of Lot's spiritual decline. Yes, Lot is considered a righteous man, but he has decided to seek the best of both worlds. He wants all the comfort of heaven and salvation, but at the same time he wants all the temporal joys and benefits of a world that is doomed for destruction. Because of wanting his feet in both worlds, Lot's spiritual decline brings on a destructive insensitivity to the things of God.

Destructive Insensitivity

We see the destructive insensitivity revealed in how Lot responds to the heavenly visitors in the beginning of the chapter.

> Now the two angels came to Sodom in the evening as Lot was sitting in the gate of Sodom. When Lot saw them, he rose to meet them and bowed down with his face to the ground. And he said, "Now behold, my lords, please turn aside into your servant's house, and spend the night, and wash your feet; then you may rise early and go on your

> way." They said however, "No, but we shall spend the night in the square." Yet he urged them strongly, so they turned aside to him and entered his house; and he prepared a feast for them, and baked unleavened bread and they ate. (Genesis 19:1–3)

The hospitality Lot shows to the two angels is indicative of his righteous character. It was customary to show hospitality to guests. When you compare Lot's hospitality to the hostility of the men of Sodom toward the guest, you see the vast contrast between them, despite the fact that Lot had declined spiritually.

However when you compare Lot's hospitality to Abraham's hospitality in Genesis 18, you begin to see that Lot was insensitive to the presence of God. The first indication of this destructive insensitivity is revealed in how Lot addresses the two angels in verse 2: "Now behold, my lord ..." Compare this address with Abraham's in Genesis 18:3: "My Lord, if now I have found favor in your sight, please do not pass your servant by." Abraham's response clearly revealed that he understood this visitation as divine. He was sensitive to the Lord's presence. It's a different story with Lot. He in essence calls the two angels "sirs." When we give into the gradual process of spiritual decline and we become entangled with the lust of the flesh, the lust of the eyes, and the pride of life, we become desensitized to the presence of God in our life.[136]

Dietrich Bonhoeffer, a German theologian who lived during the time of Hitler, gave a great commentary on this destructive insensitivity that comes from giving into the sensual and sinful desires of the flesh.

> In our members there is a slumbering inclination towards desire which is both sudden and fierce. With irresistible power, desire seizes mastery over

---

[136]Sailhamer 171.

> the flesh. All at once a secret, smoldering fire is kindled. The flesh burns and is in flames. It makes no difference whether it is sexual desire or ambition or vanity or desire for revenge or love of fame and power or greed for money, or finally, that strange desire for the beauty of the world, of nature. Joy in God is extinguished in us and we seek all our joy in the creature. At this moment God is quite unreal to us, he loses all reality, and only desire of the creature is real. We are filled, not with hatred of God, but forgetfulness of God.[137]

When we are carried away by temptation we become dangerously insensitive to the presence of God in our life. When this takes place, it then leads to destructive compromise.

Destructive Compromise

Lot's destructive insensitivity led him to a destructive compromise, a compromise that would affect his life in many ways. As Lot gave into and was led by his worldly lust, he would begin to compromise his very own righteous convictions. Scripture tells us in 2 Peter that Lot was disturbed by the sinfulness within the city of Sodom. It literally "vexed" his soul day and night. Even though he was displeased with the sinfulness of the city, he would still become a prominent leader sitting at the gate and upholding the unrighteous laws that governed the city. Instead of sitting at the gate enjoying the acceptance of the people, Lot should have stood there proclaiming the righteousness of the Lord, being concerned about pleasing God, not man. But Lot chose to follow the way of the world and

---

[137]Swindoll 566.

compromise his righteous convictions, thereby compromising his character.

After the heavenly guests entered Lot's house to enjoy his hospitality, we are told that Lot would receive some other visitors from within the city. Notice verse 4: "Before they lay down, the men of the city, the men of Sodom, surrounded the house, young and old, all the people from every quarter; and they called to Lot and said to him, 'Where are the men who came to you tonight? Bring them out to us that we may have relations with them." You see the perversity of the city in these verses. Men, both old and young, wanted to have sexual relations with the two angels, whom they thought were men.

Lot found himself in a complicated situation. He had to make a choice. He could comply with the request and let them have the men or he could refuse the request and stand up for righteousness. Lot chose to protect his guests, but he did not stand up for righteousness. Instead he made a proposal that would truly be a compromise of his righteous character. "Now, behold, I have two daughters who have not had relations with man; please let me bring them out to you, and do to them whatever you like; only do nothing to these men, inasmuch as they have come under the shelter of my roof" (Genesis 19:8). Protecting the guests was noble, but sacrificing his two virgin daughters can hardly be considered a quality of a holy and righteous character. The only moral choice in this situation would have been to stand up for righteousness and not give into unrighteousness. Lot's spiritual decline compromised his righteous convictions and righteous character. For Lot and for us, the destructive compromise of spiritual decline brings about a destructive influence to those around us.

Destructive Influence

Lot had a great opportunity to be the salt of the earth and the light of the world in Sodom and Gomorrah, but that opportunity passed when he started that downward spiral to destruction. Had the Lord called Lot to Sodom we might have a different story concerning Lot's influence, but because Lot was led to Sodom by his own worldly desires, he failed to be a positive influence to the inhabitants of the city. Instead, he became a destructive influence to the city of Sodom. Even worse, Lot would become a destructive influence upon his own family.

After the men of Sodom refused the daughters of Lot, they began to try to overtake Lot and his guests. The text tells us in verse 11 that the two angels struck the men of the city with blindness so they could not find the door. The two men then told Lot of the coming judgment upon the city and that he needed to get his family out as quickly as possible. As Lot tried to get his family together, you begin to see that Lot lost his righteous influence over his own family on account of his spiritual decline. Notice what verses 12 through 14 tell us.

> Then the two men said to Lot, "Whom else have you here? A son-in-law, and your sons and your daughters, and whomever you have in the city, bring them out of the place; for we are about to destroy this place, because their outcry has become so great before the Lord that the Lord has sent us to destroy it." Lot went out and spoke to his sons-in-law, who were to marry his daughters and said, "Up, get out of this place, for the Lord will destroy the city." But he appeared to his sons-in-law to be jesting.

Lot's spiritual decline kept him from having a positive influence upon his sons-in-law, so much so that they thought he was joking.

The reason he had lost his influence is clearly stated by Lot's actions in verse 16. After the two angels came to Lot's house the next morning and warned Lot and his family to leave the city without any hesitation, we are told, "But he hesitated."

Lot, knowing that the city was about to come under judgment hesitated because he and his family had fallen so in love with the world that it was hard to let go. The world had such a hold on them that the angels had to seize their hands and drag them out of the city. Lot wasn't rescued because he was willing to leave the city. No, Lot was rescued because the compassion of God grabbed hold of this backslidden believer and rescued him from the coming judgment. If Lot hesitated to leave the city, then you can see why he was unable to positively influence others to leave with him.

This destructive influence that Lot had would even affect the behavior of those who left the city with him. In verse 17, Lot and his family are commanded to hurry and go to the mountains and not to look back. Well, ignoring this command proved destructive to Lot's wife, "But his wife, from behind him, looked back, and she became a pillar of salt" (Genesis 19:26). Lot hesitated to leave, but his poor wife inwardly refused to leave. She became another casualty of the destructive influence of Lot's spiritual decline.

Spiritual decline brings about a destructive insensitivity, a destructive compromise, and a destructive influence. But Lot's story does not end there, for in verses 30 through 38 we see that the spiritual decline has a destructive demise.

Destructive Demise

There is a great deal of irony in these last eight verses of Genesis 19. The two virgin daughters that Lot was so willing to sacrifice to the men of Sodom would end up sleeping with Lot in an incestuous encounter. Both daughters would become pregnant and both would give birth to sons. Finding Lot in an incestuous relationship is enough proof to show the destructive demise of those who love the world more than the Lord. But even greater evidence of Lot's destructive demise is found in the two sons born to him through his own daughters. Verses 36 through 38 tell us about adversaries to the nation of Israel. "Thus both the daughters of Lot were with child by their father. The first bore a son, and called his name Moab; he is the father of the Moabites to this day. As for the younger, she also bore a son, and called his name Benammi; he is the father of the sons of Ammon to this day." These two sons would become the Moabites and the Ammonites—people who would always be the enemy of God's people. Lot could have walked by faith and not by sight and avoided this demise.

There is a Christian man in Texas who is in prison waiting to go to trial on eight federal indictments, two of which are money laundering. How did this man end up in this destructive demise? It was a gradual process. He let sin go unchecked and eventually the underlying problems came to the surface and shook his world and the world of those close to him. A Christian pharmacist in the Kansas and Missouri area is going to spend a few years in prison because he became greedy and decided to water down chemo treatments. How did he come to this destructive demise? His decline also was a gradual process.

Lot's story is a great lesson and warning for God's children. Do not love the world or anything in the world. You cannot love the world and the Lord at the same time. To avoid Lot's demise we must take a spiritual check-up every day. The only hope we have of avoiding Lot's spiritual decline is by coming to Jesus each day and asking him to give us his power to deal with those areas in our life that could lead to spiritual decline.

Some of you might already have traveled down Lot's path and you find yourself in a destructive situation on account of your worldliness. There is hope. Turn to Jesus today and he will forgive you and heal you. He may not take away the consequences, but he will make you whole again and give you a fresh start. Ask the Lord to change your heart.

Others of you are not in Lot's situation, but instead, you are in the situation that the inhabitants of Sodom found themselves in, objects of God's judgment, and what you need is the mercy of the Almighty Judge. You also have hope. Turn to Jesus from your sin and self and you can have forgiveness of sins, heaven, and eternal life.

CHAPTER XI:

FOOLISHNESS, FAITHFULNESS, AND FORGIVENESS

Genesis 20:1–18

Introduction

January often brings New Year challenges for us. Many in the church I serve decide to read through the Bible in a year. I love to hear the different comments from the people about the experience of their new challenge. The most memorable comment I heard was this one about the men and women whose lives are recorded in the Old Testament: "I have really always been a New Testament person, but I am enjoying the Old Testament because I realize that many of the great men of the faith struggled to trust in the Lord. They are by no means perfect."

We cannot truly read through the pages of the Bible without getting the sense that God's people are by no means perfect. In the Scriptures, we have men who are called "pillars of faith" and men "after God's own heart" who at times act as if they have never come to know God. What we see of the men of God in the Scriptures is true of all who start the journey of faith. The journey of faith is an upward journey, but at times it seems to be going the wrong way. One of my professors at Criswell described it well when he drew a line on the grease board as an illustration of our journey of faith. There were both high and low points on this line. The high points represented the godly times of our lives, and the low points represented the times that we strayed from the Lord.

We have already noticed this truth in Genesis 19 with the life of Lot. Lot was a righteous man who started off fine, but did not finish well. He wanted the benefits of heaven; at the same time he wanted to enjoy the desires of the heathen. This would bring his life crashing down to a destructive demise. When compared to Abraham's life, Lot's days seems to be more represented by low points than high ones. But don't think for a moment that Abraham was a perfect saint.

Just turn back to Genesis 12 to find Abraham, a great pillar of faith, failing in his journey of faith. In this beginning chapter of the life of Abraham, we find his faith faltering in the midst of trying circumstances. A famine struck the land of promise and instead of trusting the Lord to take care of him, Abraham took things into his own hands and sojourned to Egypt, resulting in a journey that would have been disastrous had it not been for the faithfulness of God.

After his rescue from his faltering faith, Abraham seemed to learn to trust in the Lord in every circumstance. Abraham trusted the Lord when he separated from his nephew Lot. He trusted the Lord when he went to fight the four kings who attacked the city of Sodom. For the most part Abraham was maturing in his faith and trust in the Lord. Abraham experienced a time of brief mistrust in the Lord in Genesis 16, but it was not a mistrust based on fear as much as it was one based on the lack of patience. Thus, from Genesis 12 up to Genesis 19, a twenty-five year period, we witness Abraham make an upward journey of faith, maturing along the way.

In Genesis 20 we will learn that though Abraham was maturing and becoming a great pillar of faith, he was also imperfect and capable of falling to the low points of life. I almost think that the Lord gave us Genesis 20 to keep us all humble before him. Remember what the apostle Paul said? The moment we think we have it together is the moment we become vulnerable to moral lapses. Abraham's life will reveal this truth once again in Genesis 20.

Some scholars argue that this is a repeat of Genesis 12; therefore, they discredit Genesis 20 as authentic. But we should not see these two chapters as duplicates; instead, we should view them as a true revelation of our humanity. Just because Abraham is making the same blunder, it does not mean the account is not authentic. What it means is that we, as humans, even redeemed beings, tend to repeat the same mistakes. That is exactly what happens in Genesis 20, a repeat mistake on the part of Abraham. Though chapters 12 and 20 of Genesis are similar, differences exist that make them each unique.

In Genesis 12 Abraham makes his way to Egypt, which is outside the Land of Promise, on account of a famine in the land. In Genesis 20 Abraham makes his way to Gerar for no other reason except by choice. Furthermore, Gerar is still within the boundaries of the Promised Land. When Abraham put his wife Sarah in danger in Genesis 12, she was barren. When Abraham put his wife in danger in Genesis 20 she was fertile.[138] Back in Genesis 18 the Lord told Abraham and Sarah that she would give birth within a year. Therefore, Sarah, though not pregnant in Genesis 20, is able to conceive. This is significant to understanding exactly what is taking place—it helps us to put into perspective the foolish actions of God's people.

The Foolish Actions of God's People

The narrative reveals the foolish actions of God's people, Abraham and Sarah, in the first two verses of Genesis 20. "Now Abraham journeyed from there toward the land of the Negev, and settled between Kadesh and Shur: then he sojourned in Gerar.

---

[138]Walton 499.

Abraham said of Sarah his wife, "She is my sister." So Abimelech king of Gerar sent and took Sarah." Abraham decided to leave his place in the oaks of Mamre and journey to a place called Gerar. The reason for the journey is not given in these verses, but it would seem that Abraham made the journey by choice, not because of circumstance. It was the famine that caused him to leave the Land of Promise and go to Egypt back in Genesis 12. It would be by Abraham's own choosing to travel from Mamre to Gerar.

Though Gerar is still within the boundaries of the Promised Land, the Philistines inhabited it. In fact, most likely Gerar was a royal city for the Philistines.[139] As Abraham made his way to Gerar, we are told in very few words that Abraham would have an encounter with the king of Gerar, Abimelech. It is interesting that the narrative does not give us any detail concerning the matter. What the narrative does tell us is that Abimelech wanted to take Sarah into his harem. "Abraham said of Sarah his wife, 'She is my sister.' So Abimelech king of Gerar sent and took Sarah."

There are two theories about why Abimelech would want to take Sarah into his harem. One theory is that the Lord restored Sarah's beauty in her latter years. Remember that she is about ninety years old at this moment in her life.[140] And if Abimelech is anything like Pharaoh, then he most likely wanted to add this beautiful woman to his harem.

The second theory, and probably the most feasible, is that Abimelech saw how prosperous Abraham was, and in an effort to ally himself with Abraham he would take his sister into his harem. This seems to fit the text better than the first conjecture.

Abraham and Sarah's foolish actions are found in their deception concerning their marriage. By deceiving Abimelech, they would put God's plan of redemption in jeopardy. When God called Abraham, he promised him that Abraham would be a

---

[139]Waltke 285.
[140]Waltke 285.

blessing to all the nations. The way in which Abraham would become a blessing is found in the fact that the Savior of the world, Jesus Christ, would come from his offspring. The foolish act of deception in these verses, without the sovereign intervention of the Lord, would have jeopardized God's eternal plan of salvation.

Satan is one reason we see God's plan of redemption being jeopardized. Satan does not want God's plan of redemption to come about because it would mean that the power of sin and death would be conquered. Therefore, Satan is going to do all he can to foil the plan of God's redemption. How would he do that? He would do so by appealing to weaknesses in the blessing bearer's life. The text reveals three areas of weakness in Abraham's life—flaws that all God's people can relate to—that would bring about the foolish actions we see in this chapter of Genesis.

The Fear of Man

In his own words and after Abimelech rebuked him, Abraham revealed the three motives of his foolish actions. In Genesis 20:11 Abraham said, "Because I thought, surely there is no fear of God in this place, and they will kill me because of my wife." Here, his foolish act of deception is the fear of man instead of the fear of God. The irony of this verse is that Abraham is guilty of what he judged Abimelech to be. Abraham feared Abimelech instead of fearing the Lord. Abraham was more concerned about what Abimelech could do to him instead of what the Lord could do to him. Fear has a way of causing God's people to do foolish things.

The Rationalization of Sin

Verse 12 gives us a second reason for such a foolish act. "Besides, she actually is my sister, the daughter of my father, but not the daughter of my mother, and she became my wife." What Abraham confessed to Abimelech was that he only told him a half-lie. Abraham rationalized his sin. Though Sarah was Abraham's half sister, his first responsibility to Sarah was as husband, not brother.

By rationalizing his foolish act of deception, Abraham put in jeopardy the purity of the marriage relationship. "But God came to Abimelech in a dream at night, and said to him, 'Behold your are a dead man because of the woman you have taken, for she is married' " (Genesis 20:3). Had it not been for divine intervention, Abimelech would have committed adultery with Sarah. God kept the purity of the marriage.

The Lingering of Flesh

The third reason for Abraham's foolish action is found in Genesis 20:13. "And it came about, when God caused me to wander from my father's house, that I said to her, 'This is the kindness you will show to me: everywhere we go, say of me, "He is my brother." Here we have the lingering of the flesh. Abraham, some twenty-five years before, made a pact with his wife Sarah soon after he journeyed from his father's house, and the pact was to lie about their relationship. This was done for the protection of Abraham's life. And it explains why Abraham and Sarah would make the same mistake again; they would hold onto the lingering flesh of distrust. They had not learned to fully trust in the Lord to take care of them.

Abraham, on account of his fear of man, rationalization of sin, and his lingering flesh, would put into jeopardy God's plan of redemption and the blessings that would come through Abraham. Abraham because of his foolish actions would move from being faithful to unfaithful. Fortunately, God's eternal plan is not dependent on man. In fact, the foolish actions of God's people are always covered by the faithful actions of God's providence.

The Faithful Actions of God's Providence

We see God's faithfulness revealed in his intervention within the situation that Abraham had caused by his foolish actions. If you look at verse 3 again you will see the nature of God's intervention. "But God said to Abimelech in a dream at night, and said to him, 'Behold, you are a dead man because of the woman whom you have taken, for she is married.' " The Lord appeared to Abimelech in a dream. As the Lord revealed to Abimelech the dire situation that he was in, he would then begin to defend his integrity in the matter. The defense offered is based upon Abimelech's ignorance in the situation.

The Honest Ignorance

After the Lord revealed the situation to Abimelech in a dream, he would make his case for honest ignorance, but before he does, Abimelech appealed to the righteous character of God. We read in verse 4, "Now Abimelech had not come near her; and he said, 'Lord, will you slay a nation, even though blameless?'" These words are very similar to the words of Abraham back in Genesis 18:23, "Will you indeed sweep away the righteous with the wicked?" Abimelech understood whom he was talking to and therefore he appealed to the righteous character of the Lord. After Abimelech made his appeal to the Lord for mercy on account of his righteous character, he then would confess the honest ignorance of the situation he was in.

Verse 5 tells us, "Did he not himself say to me, 'She is my sister'? and she herself said, 'He is my brother.' In the integrity of my heart and the innocence of my hands I have done this." Abimelech pleaded his case of honest ignorance in the situation at hand. Why was Abimelech in such a situation? Because of Abraham and Sarah's foolish acts. Abraham and Sarah's sins not only jeopardized the plan of God through Abraham, but also caused the possibility of disastrous consequences for those who were brought into the situation in honest ignorance.

What is especially important concerning the honest ignorance of Abimelech is that he did not have sexual relations with Sarah. Verse 4 tells us, "Now Abimelech had not come near her." Had Abimelech come near Sarah, she possibly would have given birth to Abimelech's heir and not to Abraham's. You can see how the foolish actions jeopardized the plan of God. But more importantly than the fact that Abimelech did not have sexual relations with Sarah is the fact that the faithful actions of God's providence intervened in the situation.

The Faithful Intervention

We see the faithful intervention of the Lord in this situation revealed in the Lord's response to Abimelech. "Then God said to him in the dream, 'Yes, I know that in the integrity of your heart you have done this." (Genesis 20:6). Let me stop and just point out that God acknowledges that Abimelech's sin is done out of ignorance, not presumption. After Abimelech acknowledged his honest ignorance, God revealed the faithful intervention in the situation, "And I also kept you from sinning against me; therefore I did not let you touch her" (Genesis 20:6).

This statement on the part of the Lord is a profound one. Had it not been for the faithful action of the Lord, Abimelech would have slept with Sarah. Yes, in ignorance Abimelech acted, but God's faithful intervention kept him from truly sinning against God. Have you ever thought about God's faithfulness in terms of how much sin he keeps us from? Think about how many times in our lives God faithfully intervened in a situation to keep us from sinning against him. I know of times in my Christian life where I was sure that God faithfully intervened to keep me from going down a path I would later regret.

Why would God intervene in the foolish acts of his people in Genesis 20? He would intervene because he had a promise to keep. The Lord promised Abraham and Sarah that they would have a child, and from him would come kings and nations. More importantly, from him would come the King of kings and the Lord of lords. This promise was not dependent upon man, but upon God himself. Therefore, though Abraham and Sarah were unfaithful, God would remain faithful to his character, his promise, and his reputation by faithfully intervening in the foolish actions of his people's lives.

When Napoleon was making his march toward the city of Moscow, he decided to share his plans of conquer to a certain lady. As he shared his plans, he did so with a prideful and arrogant attitude. The lady quickly rebuked him and said, "Sir, be more reverent. You must remember that man proposes, but God disposes." Napoleon responded back in his haughtiness, "Madam, not only do I propose, but I also dispose." Those words would come back to haunt him. In a matter of months, after retreating from the burned-out city, he found himself engaged in a battle with frost and snow, a battle that would wreck his army and his prestige, and that would eventually send him as a defeated exile to the prison of St. Helena.[141]

Abraham proposed to wreck God's plan of redemption through his foolish actions, but God still disposes. The fulfillment of God's plan is not dependent upon man's faithfulness, but on God's faithfulness through his providential hand.

It is encouraging to know that even when we give into the foolish actions as God's people and sin against God; he is still faithful to his covenant. This we see in God's faithful intervention in this narrative. But even more encouraging in this

---

[141]Green 174.

text than the faithful actions of God is the forgiving attitude of God's personality.

The Forgiving Attitude of God's Personality

The forgiving attitude of God's personality is displayed in how the Lord deals with both Abimelech and Abraham. Though Abimelech sins out of honest ignorance, the Lord would still hold him accountable and responsible for his sin. In fact, the Lord told Abimelech that until Sarah was restored to her husband, he and his household were still under the penalty of death. Notice what the Lord says in Genesis 20:7: "Now therefore, restore the man's wife, for he is a prophet, and he will pray for you and you will live. But if you do not restore her, know that you shall surely die, you and all who are yours." Abimelech's first choice to take Sarah was done in honest ignorance, but if he failed to restore Sarah to Abraham, his sin would be a sin of willful disobedience.

Verses 8 and following show us that Abimelech took the words of the Lord seriously. Abimelech woke the next morning, gathered around his servants, and told them all that had happened. Abimelech then found Abraham and confronted him. "Then Abimelech called Abraham and said to him, 'What have you done to us? And how have I sinned against you, that you have brought on me and on my kingdom a great sin? You have done to me things that ought not to be done'" (Genesis 20:9). This is not only a direct confrontation of Abraham's sin from Abimelech; it is also an indirect rebuke of Abraham's sin from the Lord. After Abraham was confronted, in verses 11 through 13 he confessed the source of his sins: the fear of man, the rationalization of sin, and the lingering of flesh.

Abimelech then made good on what the Lord told him to do back in verse 7, and he restored Sarah back to Abraham as well as blessed them with material goods. "Abimelech then took sheep and oxen and male and female servants, and gave them to Abraham, and restored his wife Sarah to him." Here is the fruit of

Abimelech's confession before the Lord, the restoration of Sarah to her husband.

And the Lord did exactly what he said he would do if Abimelech confessed and complied with the demands of the Lord, "Abraham prayed to God, and God healed Abimelech and his wife and his maids, so they bore children. For the Lord had closed fast all the wombs of the household of Abimelech because of Sarah, Abraham's wife." We see God's forgiving attitude demonstrated in how he dealt with Abimelech. The Lord could have killed Abimelech from the start, but he didn't. Instead God gave Abimelech an opportunity to confess his sin, and the Lord forgave him.

God's forgiveness is also revealed by how God dealt with Abraham. We never once see God defend Abraham's sin, but we do see him defend and protect Abraham on the basis of his own faithfulness.[142] The Lord did not appear directly to Abraham, but indirectly through the confrontation of Abimelech, and Abraham came clean and confessed the reasons for his foolish activities in the first place. Had not Abraham confessed his sin, the prayer that he prayed in verse 17 would not have been heard, for the Bible tells us that if we cherish sin in our hearts the Lord will not hear us. The Lord heard Abraham and he healed Abimelech.

D.L. Moody, in one of his great evangelistic sermons, told this story of his life growing up. When Moody was only four his father died, leaving him and his siblings to help their mom. Soon after the death of their father, Moody's eldest brother decided to run away from home. Moody remembered hearing his mother praying late at night for the safe return of his brother. Every day his mother would have him walk to the post office to see if any letter or word had come from or about his brother. So consumed with the missing brother was Moody's mom that his siblings began to question her love for them. One day a knock came at the door and it was the eldest brother. Moody's mom greeted the son saying, "Is it possible that my son has come home? Come in."

[142]Wiersbe 91.

But before the eldest brother went in he said to his mother, "Mom, I can't come in until you forgive me of what I have done to you!" She rushed and put her arms around the boy and said, "I forgive you." After telling this story, D.L. Moody then told his congregation, "My friends, this forgiveness is nothing to the sin that your heavenly father wants you to confess to him. Oh that you would be wise to come to him now while he is still willing."[143]

This text reveals the condition of us all. We are like Abraham and Abimelech who have committed sin against a holy God. Fortunately we cannot sin more than God can forgive. "When it comes to a battle between sin and grace, God's grace wins every time. When we sin, we sin as humans, finite creatures, but when God forgives he does so as an infinite creator."[144]

---

[143]Elon Foster, *6000 Classic Sermon Illustrations* (Grand Rapids: Baker, 1993) 354.
[144]Carter 80.

CHAPTER XII:

KEYS TO CHRISTIAN LIVING

Genesis 21:1–21

Introduction

During World War I, one of our American airmen took off from an airfield located in Kobar, Arabia. Little did the pilot know that while the plane was on the ground a large rat had crawled inside the cockpit. While in the air the pilot heard a gnawing sound behind him. He immediately realized a rodent was onboard. Alarmed at what could turn into a disastrous situation, the pilot remembered that rats could not live in high altitudes. So the pilot did the smart thing and pointed his airplane up and climbed to altitudes where breathing was difficult. After some time at the high altitude, the gnawing stopped. When he landed on the ground he found that that the gnawing rat had died.[145]

The gnawing rat represents well the many gnawing struggles that we face daily in our Christian walk. Many, if not all, of the gnawing struggles that we face can be dealt with much like the pilot dealt with the gnawing rat, by climbing to greater altitudes in our Christian walk.

---

[145]Zuck 69.

The last two chapters in the studies of Genesis 19 and 20 have revealed to us what happens when we don't move to higher altitudes in our Christian living. We saw gnawing struggles bring Lot to a destructive demise. We saw gnawing struggles bring Abraham to a point of jeopardizing God's eternal plan and the purity of his marriage. Fortunately, God is faithful when we are not and he intervened in Abraham's situation. But even more importantly, he demonstrated his forgiving attitude to a saint who had gone astray.

Now, one could take a fatalistic view of the journey of faith when we observe the lives of Lot and Abraham. If our journey of faith is going to be characterized by high points and low points, then why try? Why not take the "Que sera, sera" attitude and say, "What ever will be, will be"? The answer is simple; God does not want us to take that approach to our Christian living. Yes, we will have low points, and yes the Lord will forgive us, but God has given us everything we need to live the Christian life. Though the Christian life includes gnawing struggles, we can eliminate many of them if we will just rise to higher altitudes in our walk. We can avoid the mishaps of Lot and Abraham if we have a basic understanding of the Christian life. We can spend more time at the high points and less at the low by having some fundamental knowledge of Christian living and by appropriating it. Genesis 21 gives us some fundamental truths concerning the Christian walk.

It is hard to believe that a chapter which declares the birth of a promised child and the expulsion of a problem child can give us some fundamental truth concerning our Christian walk, but it does. There are three keys to Christian living that I would like to share with you, keys that are found in the first twenty-one verses of Genesis 21. From God's standpoint the keys deal with the promises of God, the precepts of God, and the power of God. From the standpoint of the child of God the keys deal with trust, obedience, and yielding.

This chapter is designed to be very practical in nature. Some might have read the last two chapters of this book wondering how to avoid Lot's demise or how to steer clear of the foolish ways of Abraham? The answers to these questions are crucial. If we are going to have more high points than low points in our journey of faith, then we must learn to appropriate the first key, which is to rely on the unfailing nature of the promises of God.

Rely on the Unfailing Nature of the Promises of God

Since the beginning of our study of the life of Abraham we have been anticipating the promise of God to Abraham concerning an heir. The Lord told Abraham when he called him that he would be a great nation. This is all fine and dandy, but Abraham's wife was barren and they were up in their years. Still, the Lord promised to Abraham and Sarah that she would give birth to a son, and through Abraham's offspring would come kings and nations, but more importantly, through Abraham's offspring would come the Savior of the world, Jesus Christ.

For ten chapters in Genesis we have been anticipating the promise of a child. These ten chapters of the life of Abraham represent twenty-five or so years of his life. The Lord gave Abraham and Sarah a promise and they would have to wait for God to fulfill that promise. Now, the day of God's fulfillment has finally come. Genesis 21 records the Lord's promise being fulfilled. The scene is set for us. "Then the Lord took note of Sarah as he had said, and the Lord did for Sarah as he had promised. So Sarah conceived and bore a son to Abraham in his old age, at the appointed time of which God had spoken to him" (Genesis 21:1–2).

It is amazing that within these two verses we have about a nine- or ten-month period. Sarah, who was barren, was now fertile and she conceived and gave birth to a son in her old age. The fact that she was fertile illustrates once again how

Abraham's foolish actions in Genesis 20 jeopardized the plan of God, but thanks be to God who intervened. In the beginning of Genesis 21 we again find divine visitation taking place, but for different reasons than we read about in Genesis 19.

The Divine Visitation

A verb is used in verse 1 that we need to take note of to really grasp what the Lord is doing in these two verses. That Hebrew word is "paw-kad." In English we translate that verb "took note" or "visited," with an emphasis of grace. The verb "paw-kad," as it is used in this context, has the idea of divine intervention for the purpose of good. God is intervening in the life of Sarah for the purpose of blessing her with a son.[146] The same verb "paw-kad" is used one other time in the book of Genesis. In Genesis 50:24, Joseph uses "paw-kad" to announce that the Lord would visit his people in Egypt and deliver them from the bondage of slavery. Both cases speak of divine intervention for the purpose of good. In both instances the destiny of God's people was changed.[147]

Elsewhere in the Old Testament, "paw-kad" is used to describe how the Lord intervened in the life a Hannah, another barren woman, and caused her to conceive and give birth to Samuel. "Paw-kad" is used in Ruth 1 to describe how the Lord had visited his people. This visitation would send Naomi and Ruth back to Israel after a sojourn in Moab, and would bring Ruth and Boaz together in marriage. In all these cases the Lord intervened in the lives of his people for the purpose of good, and this divine intervention for the purpose of good would alter the destiny of God's people. This is true of God's visitation to Sarah, to Israel in Egypt, to Hannah, and to his people during the time of Ruth. At the heart of the divine visitation in these two verses is the unwavering nature of the promises of God.[148]

---

[146]Ross 378.
[147]Ross 378.
[148]Ross 378.

The Unwavering Nature of the Promises of God

The reason for the visitation is stated three times within the two verses. Pay attention to these verses again. "Then the Lord took note of Sarah as he had said, and the Lord did for Sarah as he had promised. So Sarah conceived and bore a son to Abraham in his old age, at the appointed time of which God had spoken to him."

We are told in verse one "as he had said" and "as he had promised." We are told in verse two "God had spoken to him." When you see something repeated, especially three times within two verses, you need to take note of what is being repeated because the repetition stresses the importance of what is being said.

Why did God visit Sarah? Why did she conceive and give birth to a son? The answer is found in the repetition: God said he would do it and therefore he did it. The repetition of the spoken word of God as the reason for such visitation reveals the total reliability of the word of God and the total reliability of God's promises. If God says he will do something, then you can be assured he will. The Lord did exactly what he said he would do concerning Abraham and Sarah. He said that he would give them a son in their old age, and he did. He said that he would do it at his appointed time, not at man's, and he did. God's promises are absolute.

The first key to Christian living is learning to trust and rely on the sure promises of God. Most of our gnawing struggles can be overcome by simply trusting in the word of God and the promises of God. We move to a higher altitude when we put our confidence in God's word. Think about how this key could have prevented Abraham from giving into some of his gnawing struggles. If Abraham had trusted in God's promise to take care of him, then he could have avoided the sojourn into Egypt. If Abraham had trusted in the Lord and his timing, he could have avoided having a child with his wife's servant Hagar, a child that would become an historic problem. If Abraham had trusted in the promises of God he would not have given into the foolish actions we witnessed in Genesis 20. You can see from Abraham's life just how important it is to trust in the promises of God. Relying on the promises of God calms our fears, and brings joy to our sorrowed heart and confidence when circumstances become difficult. We must rely on the promises of God to have peace for a troubled heart.

A good illustration of relying on the promises of God is found in a discussion that Jesus had with his disciples in John 14:1 just before he went to the cross. Jesus told his disciples, "Let not your heart be troubled, believe in God, believe also in me." Jesus gives us a command here, "Let not your heart be troubled." This command is in the passive voice. Therefore it is not something we do so much as it is something that must be done to us. God is the only one who can calm a troubled heart; therefore, our role in fulfilling this command is found in the exhortation to believe in God and his son Jesus Christ. When we trust in Jesus we have the promise of heaven. When we trust in Jesus we have the promise of salvation. When we trust in Jesus we have the promise of his return. And trusting in these promises can bring calm to a troubled heart.

A practical way of relying on the promises of God is to view the promises of God as a checkbook. "When you come across a promise, sign that promise by faith, then present that signed check and God's great bank of grace, and you will come away enriched with a present help in a time of need."[149] Relying on the unwavering promises of God is crucial in rising to higher altitudes in your Christian living. The second key, just as important for climbing higher in our Christian living, deals with how we respond to the requirements of the precepts of God.

---

[149]Carter 168.

Respond to the Requirements of the Precepts of God

Abraham and Sarah's response to the fulfillment of God's promise shows us the second key to Christian living. In their response, we see how important it is that God's people respond to God's faithfulness by means of joyfully obeying his precepts. In verses 3 through 5 we see the expression of obedience as well as the expression of joy.

The Expression of Obedience

The expression of obedience is the first thing we see. "Abraham called the name of his son who was born to him, whom Sarah bore to him, Isaac. Then Abraham circumcised his son Isaac when he was eight days old, as God had commanded him. Now Abraham was one hundred years old when his son Isaac was born to him" (Genesis 21:3–4).

Before we focus on the expression of obedience that we see in these verses, it would be wise to look at the repetition. The phrase "his son" and the name "Isaac" are repeated three times. The repetition points us to the fact that the Lord had done exactly what he said he would do. It stressed the fact that God has been faithful to his word.

It would also be wise for us to remember the significance of the name Isaac at this time. The name Isaac means "to laugh," and it takes us back to Genesis 17 and 18. It was there that the Lord reaffirmed his promise of a son to Abraham and Sarah. When the Lord told Abraham and Sarah about the promised child, they both laughed because of their age. The Lord then told Abraham that he was to name the son Isaac. And in response to God's faithfulness, Abraham did exactly what the Lord commanded him to do back in Genesis 17; he named his son Isaac. Abraham responded to God's faithfulness in fulfilling his promises by obeying the requirements of God's precepts.

Not only do we see the expression of obedience revealed in the naming of Abraham's son, but we also see it revealed in the circumcision of his son, "Then Abraham circumcised his son Isaac when he was eight days old, as God had commanded him." The Lord commanded Abraham back in Genesis 17 as well that he needed to circumcise the males of his household, for this was a sign of the covenant between God and Abraham and Abraham's descendants.

If you look at the end of verse 4 you will see what he did, for there it says, "as God had commanded him." Abraham responded to the requirements of the precepts of God. Now, look back at verse 1 with me; notice the last phrase, "as he had promised." The phrases in verse 1 and 4 are grammatically similar, and for a reason. The Lord was faithful to his promise as we see in verse 1, and therefore Abraham, in response to God's faithfulness, would be faithful to God's precepts in verse 4. We see Abraham's response to the requirements of the precepts of God in verses 3 through 5. In verses 6 through 8 we see the joyful attitude in which Abraham and Sarah obeyed God's precepts.

The Expression of Joy

The joyful expression of Abraham and Sarah's response to God's precepts is found in Sarah's declaration in verse 6. "Sarah said, 'God has made laughter for me; everyone who hears will laugh with me.' " There is a play on the name Isaac here. Sarah doesn't see the name Isaac as a constant reminder of her doubt concerning the promises of God, but instead she joyfully declares that the birth of Isaac would be a constant reminder of God's faithfulness to his promises, and the constant reminder of his faithfulness will be a source of joyful obedience.

I want you to think about something for a moment. If Abraham and Sarah responded to God's faithfulness to his promises with joyful obedience and devotion, how much more should God's people who live on the fulfilled side of the cross respond to God's faithfulness with joyful obedience and devotion? All of God's promises are fulfilled in the death and resurrection of Jesus Christ. Christians should respond to that faithfulness by joyfully obeying the precepts of God. In responding to the requirements of God's precepts we in essence tell the Lord that we love him for all he as done. It is paramount that we trust in the unwavering promises of God, but just as important, we must also joyfully obey his precious precepts.

A third key to Christian living revealed in these verses is just as significant as the first two. In fact, you cannot truly rise to higher altitudes apart from appropriating all three keys. The third key, found in verses 9 through 21, shows the need for Christians to remove impediments to the power of God.

Remove the Impediments to the Power of God

A little problem arises as Abraham and Sarah are celebrating the arrival of God's promised son. We see the problem arising in verse 9, "Now Sarah saw the son of Hagar the Egyptian, whom she had borne to Abraham, mocking." The problem is going to come from Ishmael, Abraham's son from Sarah's servant. Sadly, that this problem would not have happened had Sarah and Abraham trusted in the promises of God.

Seeing that a problem might arise, Sarah made a demand of Abraham. "Therefore she said to Abraham, 'Drive out this maid and her son, for the son of this maid shall not be an heir with my son Isaac." At issue in her demand is the heir; therefore, the only real solution and protection of Isaac in being the heir is by getting rid of Hagar and Ishmael. However, this would disturb Abraham because Ishmael was still his son. But the Lord would confirm the need to remove Ishmael from the scene. God had already promised that Abraham's descendants would be named through Isaac. To protect this promise the Lord would have Abraham remove the threat to the promise. The blessings of God would come through Isaac; therefore, the Lord would have

Abraham remove the impediment to that blessing, and that impediment was Ishmael.

Abraham did exactly what the Lord told him to do; he sent Hagar and Ishmael walking. But don't think for a moment that God had abandoned Hagar and Ishmael. Don't think for a second that the Lord did not take care of them. In the next verses we see once again the Lord being faithful to his promises. Back in Genesis 16 the Lord told Hagar that he would take care of her and Ishmael, and he keeps his promise in verses 15 through 21. Furthermore, God's care for Hagar and Ishmael shows how much the Lord loves the outcast and rejected.

So the Lord had Abraham remove the threat to the blessings of God that would come through Isaac. But how does this situation translate into the third key to Christian living? How does this situation reveal the need for God's people to remove the impediments to God's power in their life? The answer to these questions is found in the New Testament.

In Galatians 4, Paul used Genesis 21 and the two children of Abraham—Isaac and Ishmael—as an allegory to illustrate an aspect of the Christian life. Paul said, "For it is written that Abraham had two sons, one by the bondwoman and one by the free woman. But the son of the bondwoman was born of the flesh, and the son by the free woman though the promise. This is allegorically speaking" (Galatians 4:22–24). Now, move down a few verses in Galatians to read, "And you brethren, like Isaac, are children of promise. But as at that time he who was born according to the flesh persecuted him who was born according to the Spirit, so it is now also" (vv. 28–29). Paul is referring to Genesis 21 where we find Ishmael "mocking" Isaac. The conflict between Ishmael and Isaac is an allegory to the conflict between the flesh and the Spirit.

What is the solution to the conflict between flesh and Spirit? Paul goes on to tell us by quoting Genesis 21:10, "But what does the scripture say? 'Cast out the bondwoman and her son, for the son of the bondwoman shall not be heir with the son of the free woman." These were the words of Sarah, and Paul likens the removal of Ishmael with the removal of the flesh. Why the removal of the flesh? If you go on to read Galatians 5, Paul speaks about walking in the Spirit versus walking in the flesh. If we are going to walk in the Spirit, that is, if we are going to walk in the power of God, then we must remove the impediments to the Spirit of God in our lives. What is the impediment to the power of God in our lives? The impediment is the flesh, that which belongs to the old nature.

If you are going to live the Christian life successfully and move to higher altitudes in your Christian experience, then you must yield to the Spirit of God in your life. You must yield to the power of God in your life. You must also remove the impediments to the power of God, which is all that belongs to the flesh. I encourage you to read Galatians 5 so you can understand that which is of the flesh and that which is of the Spirit.

On June 12, 1979, a man made aviation history when he flew his pedal-powered aircraft across the English Channel. He took off from England and flew for three hours some fifteen feet above the water until he finally made his destination some twenty-miles later in France. As amazing as this achievement was, man-powered flight will never be practical because man cannot put out the needed power to maintain extended flights.[150]

In the same way, no one can truly live the Christian life in his or her own strength and power. The only way we can live the Christian life and climb to higher altitudes in our Christian experience is through the enabling power of God that comes from the Spirit of God. It is only by the enabling power of the Holy Spirit that one can live the Christian life. We must remove the impediments and yield to the power of God in our lives.

The keys for Christian living are grounded in the promises of God, the precepts of God, and the power of God. Christians must trust the promises of God, obey the precepts of God, and yield to the power of God if they are going to climb above those gnawing struggles in life. When you rely on these

---

[150]Green 56.

three keys then will you be successful in your daily Christian living.

CHAPTER XIII:

CHRISTIANS MAKING A DIFFERENCE IN THE COMMUNITY

Genesis 21:22–34

Introduction

One of the great debates consuming our society today is the debate over the separation of church and state. The debate finds its source in a statement made by Thomas Jefferson in the 1800s concerning the "wall of separation." Some argue that the "wall of separation" Jefferson referred to when he wrote to Baptists in Connecticut was the separation between church and state. Others argue Jefferson was referring to the "wall of separation" between the federal government and state governments.[151] Needless to say, today we have many people spending a great deal of energy to keep the sacred with the sacred and the secular with the secular.

The problem often found in church and state relations is how the two view one another. When it comes to the secular, Christians often have the perspective of the government as an evil empire. This perspective is often generated by what the

[151]David Holwick, *Holwick's Sermon Data Base.* (This story came from Chuck Colson's Ministry.)

Scriptures declare about the secular government. On one hand, you have the state being described as controlled by demonic powers. The apostle Paul said, "For our struggle is not against flesh and blood, but against the rulers, against the powers, against the world forces of this darkness, against the spiritual forces of wickedness in the heavenly places" (Ephesians 6:12). In the book of Revelation we find the godless government at its worst destined for destruction.[152] On the other hand, the Scriptures clearly declare the government in a positive light. The apostle Paul tells us the government is ordained and authorized by God and Christians are to obey the authorities of the secular government for that very reason (Romans 13:1–7).

Here is the reality of this seeming contradiction. God established the secular government and at times it will function as God intends, but at other times it functions as God never intended. The secular government is much like the sacred church. The church, also established by God, at times functions as a blessing to all, but at other times the God-established church acts like the devil and brings misery on many.[153]

With all this said, how do we as Christians make a difference in a secular society? How do we impact the secular with the sacred? How do we keep ourselves from one extreme of isolationism and the other extreme of secularism? The last thirteen verses of Genesis 21 give us some great insight into answering these questions.

In these verses we have two characters, Abraham and Abimelech. This is not the first time we have met Abimelech in our study of the life of Abraham. In Genesis 20 we were introduced to Abimelech on account of the foolish actions of Abraham and Sarah. They lied to Abimelech about their marital situation, putting Abimelech under the judgment of God. The meeting of the two in these next verses is quite different from that first meeting.

---

[152]Boice 669.
[153]Boice 669.

The meeting of Abraham and Abimelech is significant to answering the questions that have been proposed because you have a patriarch and a prince meeting together. The sacred and the secular come together for the purpose of good. They come together in the form of a covenant, an oath taken between two parties. The situation presented in these verses enables Christians to see how we can truly make a difference in our community. It enables us to see how we can participate in the secular without losing the sacred. If Christians as individuals and as a church body are going to make a difference in our community, then we must first earn respect by means of our experience with God.

Earn Respect by Means of Your Experience with God

We see this truth demonstrated in verse 22. "Now it came about at that time that Abimelech and Phicol, the commander of his army, spoke to Abraham, saying, 'God is with you in all that you do." The period of time between Abraham and Abimelech's first meeting is debatable. Roughly three to four years have passed, enough time for Abraham and Sarah to conceive and bear a child. During this period Abimelech was able to observe the life of Abraham. Abimelech witnessed Abraham experience God in his life, and it gave him reason to respect Abraham.

Abimelech first recognized the hand of God upon Abraham back in Genesis 20. Abraham had deceived Abimelech and put him in a dangerous situation, but the Lord spoke to Abimelech in a dream and warned him about Sarah. He also said to Abimelech that Abraham was a prophet.

The second time Abimelech was aware that the Lord's hand was upon Abraham was after he confronted Abraham concerning his sin. After Abimelech restored Sarah back to Abraham, Abraham prayed for Abimelech and the Lord heard Abraham's prayer and healed the plague that had come upon

Abimelech's household. Without a doubt these two instances gave evidence to Abimelech that Abraham had an experience with God and that God was with him. I also imagine that over the three or four years that Abimelech watched Abraham live and witnessed how God blessed Abraham that he knew with surety that God was with him in all that he did.

The experience Abraham had with God would earn him respect and esteem from the pagan king Abimelech. This is especially interesting when you realize that of all people, Abimelech had every reason to disrespect Abraham. Abraham lied to Abimelech and jeopardized his life and the life of his family, and Abraham accused him of having no fear of God. All of these things could have cultivated a deep disrespect for Abraham. Abimelech could have said Abraham was nothing but a hypocrite who acted worse than he did.[154] But God restored Abraham, and God was with Abraham and blessed him in everything he did. The very presence of God earned Abraham respect with the secular ruler. As with Abraham, the evident presence of God in our daily life is by no means a liability in the arena of the secular. Instead, it is an asset that can earn us respect and favor with those who live without God.

A good illustration of this truth is found in the book of Acts. After Pentecost and Peter's great sermon, many people were saved. The church was unified, they met each other's needs, and they worshipped the Lord every day. The church was "praising God and having favor with all the people" (Acts 2:47). God's presence was upon them, which resulted in favor with all the people. Believers and unbelievers alike respected and esteemed the church on account of God's presence, on account of the experience with God that the early church had. The writer of Proverbs confirms this truth. "When a man's ways are pleasing to the Lord, he makes even his enemies to be at peace with him" (Proverbs 16:7). Eugene Patterson's contemporary paraphrase of

---

[154]Boice 669.

this verse says, "When God approves of your life, even your enemies will end up shaking your hand."[155]

Does the public notice that God is with you in all that you do? Have you earned the respect of those around you because your life is pleasing to God? When God is with us and the world notices, even the enemies of God will respect us. If we are going to make a difference in our community, then we must earn respect by means of our experience with God.

Find Common Ground to Work On

The next thing that will help us make a difference in our community is somewhat of a tall order. If we are going to make a difference in the secular, then we, the "sacred," must find a common ground to work on with those who are the secular.

Why is this a tall order for Christians? We often have the mindset that if we don't agree totally, then there is no common ground to work on. This is demonstrated well within Christendom with the many different denominations, which illustrates that we don't agree on all points. But it does not mean that we, the body of Christ, cannot find a common ground to work on with other churches.

When, for example, the Billy Graham Crusades visit a city, churches and individuals from all around the state and from all different denominations unite on a common ground, the gospel of Jesus Christ as the only means of being saved. It is possible for churches to find common ground with other churches for the purpose of glorifying the Lord. In the same manner it is possible for Christians to unite with the secular on common ground for the purpose of good. Abraham and Abimelech demonstrate this truth in Genesis 21:23–26.

---

[155]Eugene H. Peterson, *The Message: The Bible in Contemporary Language* (Colorado Springs: NavPress Publishing Group, 2002).

> "Now therefore, swear to me here by God that you will not deal falsely with me or with my offspring or with my posterity, but according to the kindness that I have shown to you, you shall show to me and to the land in which you have sojourned." Abraham said, "I swear it." But Abraham complained to Abimelech because of the well of water which the servants of Abimelech had seized. And Abimelech said, "I do not know who has done this thing; you did not tell me, nor did I hear of it until today."

In these verses we see at least two matters of interest for both parties, which provided a common ground for both of them to work on: peace and justice.

Peace

The first matter of mutual interest for both parties is that of peace.[156] Abimelech's request to Abraham was a request for a peaceful relationship between the two, since they were to coexist in the same region. Most likely the request was made out of Abimelech's self-interest and self-preservation. A little insight is given in verse 22 where it says that "Phicol, the commander of his army, spoke to Abraham." The presence of the commander of Abimelech's army indicates that Abimelech viewed Abraham as a mighty force to be reckoned with. He most likely heard about how Abraham was able to defeat the powerful kings and rescue Lot (Genesis 14). He also noticed how the Lord blessed him with prosperity and protection. He knew that Abraham and his God made one powerful team. Therefore, he would seek a covenant, a treaty between the two, that ensured peace.

---

[156]Boice 661.

Abraham responded to Abimelech's request with a mutual interest for peace when he said, "I swear it" (v. 24). This is not the first time that Abraham made a peaceful alliance with pagan kings. He did the very same thing back in Genesis 14 when he was staying in the oaks of Mamre. Peace was a praiseworthy cause, common ground that the two could work on together.

Jesus said in his great sermon on the mount, "Blessed are the peacemakers, for they shall be called sons of God." God's people should be advocates for peace within the secular government. One of the greatest testimonies that we have as Christians is to show a sinful and divided world that we can achieve peace if we work at it.[157] Of course, if the church is going to have any credibility regarding peace, then we need to begin to cultivate it within the church. Another area that would provide a common ground for prince and pagan to work on is found in Abraham's complaint to Abimelech.

Justice

While Abraham has Abimelech's ear, he voices a complaint concerning a certain issue in verse 25. "But Abraham complained to Abimelech because of the well of water which the servants of Abimelech seized." The verb complained means to "determine what is right."[158] Abraham pleaded for justice, for that is what justice is all about, "determining what is right."

One cannot have true peaceful relations without justice.[159] Here lies the second matter of mutual interest that the two could agree on: to do what is right. Abimelech, in an indirect way is going to acknowledge the injustice and do the right thing. "I do not know who has done this thing; you did not tell me, nor did I hear about it today" (v. 26). Abimelech pleaded ignorance in the situation, but he corrected the situation once it was made known

[157]Boice 672.
[158]Waltke 299.
[159]Boice 673–674.

to him. We know this to be true not because the text tells us directly, but because Abraham and Abimelech followed by cutting a covenant between them.

Christians and the secular government can come together in matters of determining what is right. Justice is a form of morality, and Christians can find different aspects of morality that are of mutual interest to both the Christian and the state. In a Christian magazine article concerning Christians in politics, the author stated that Christians and the state could find a common ground in the areas of common morality, civil morality, and social morality.

Christians are aliens in a foreign land, just like Abraham in this text, but that does not mean that we cannot come together with those of this world for praiseworthy purposes. In fact, we must find a common ground to work on if we are truly going to be the salt of the earth and the light of the world. But there is a warning to our involvement that is revealed in this text. We need to find common ground without compromising our character or principles.

Don't Compromise Your Character or Your Principles

It is one thing to find common ground in secular society for the purpose of good, but Christians must not find that common ground by compromising their character or their principles.

Character

Within these verses we have a subtle rebuke of the foolish actions that Abraham took in Genesis 20 when Abraham deceived Abimelech by telling him that Sarah was his sister and by omitting the fact that she was his wife. Abraham lied to save his neck. The fact that Abimelech had to ask for an oath from

Abraham indicated that he lacked trust in Abraham. In Genesis 21:23 Abimelech says, "Now therefore, swear to me here by God that you will not deal falsely with me or my offspring." We can see from Abimelech's words that he did not trust Abraham.

Abimelech knew that God was with Abraham and that God had restored him after his foolish deception, but he also knew that Abraham was capable of deceit. Therefore, he asked Abraham to swear by God that he would not deal falsely with him. This is a significant rebuke to Abraham. This statement on the part of Abimelech is also significant for God's people and their need to maintain a godly character.

Professing Christians have high expectations from the world. The secular expect God's people to be people of integrity, people of character. Even more importantly, God expects his people to have integrity and good character. People should be able to trust God's people on account of their character. When former President Clinton ran for office, he was questioned about his character and he responded, "Character is not the issue." I disagree. Our credibility before a secular world is established through our integrity and character. Find common ground to work on, but don't in any way compromise your character and integrity.

Principles

Just as important to our character are our principles. In fact, if you compromise your principles you in essence compromise your character. We can find common ground to work on, but not at the expense of the beliefs that we hold and cherish. We must be in the world, but not of the world. To maintain this position as God's people in the community we must realize that we will need to go our separate ways on many issues on account of our principles.

After Abraham and Abimelech made a covenant, and Abraham named the place Beersheba, we are told in verse 32,

"So they made a covenant at Beersheeba; and Abimelech and Phicol, the commander of his army, arose and returned to the land of the Philistines." Though the patriarch and the pagan found common ground to work on, their separation reveals that they were two men and two ways.[160]

The same is true of the church. We may find common ground to work on with a secular society, but the truth still remains—we are different from the world. We have different priorities, different purposes, and yes, different principles than the world. Therefore, there will be issues that divide, issues in which the church must rise up and declare, "Thus says the Lord."

The world says, "It's a choice." God's people say, "It's a life." The world says, "It's an alternative lifestyle." God's people say, "It's sinful." The world says, "It will help the economy and education." God's people say, "It will destroy lives and families." The church has a higher calling, a calling to proclaim the righteousness and justice of a holy God. Our first responsibility is not to the authorities of the world, but to the one who has the authority over the world—Jesus Christ. There are times when God's people must tell the world, "We must obey God before we obey man." We must find common ground to work on, but not at the expense of our character and our principles.

Never Forget Your Ultimate Purpose

As God's people get involved with the secular to make a difference, we must never forget our ultimate purpose. We strive for peace and justice with the secular world for a purpose and that purpose is revealed in the actions of Abraham. "Abraham planted a tamarisk tree at Beersheba, and there he called on the name of the LORD, the Everlasting God" (Genesis 21:33).

Abraham does two things in this verse: he plants a tree and he calls on the name of the Lord. Here we have a name for

---

[160]Boice 674.

God that shows up for the first time in the Bible. The Hebrew name for God here is "El-Olam." In Genesis 14 the Lord was called "El-Elyon," which means "God Most High." In Genesis 17 the Lord was called "El-Shaddai," which means "God Almighty." Now, the Lord is called "El-Olam" which means the "Eternal God," or the "Everlasting God." In planting the tree and calling upon the Lord Abraham did two things that reveal the ultimate purpose of God's people. Abraham worshipped and witnessed. He proclaimed the truth of the one true God, who is God Most High, God Almighty, and Eternal God.

The tree was a reminder of the covenant, but it was also a statement of faith that God would protect his well. The tree would be a constant reminder of God's provision of water from that well. By planting the tree Abraham was telling the whole world about the Lord—El-Olam and his faithfulness.

As Christians involved in the secular world we must not forget our ultimate purpose to be a witness of El-Olam to the world. But we don't have to plant a tree to declare the faithfulness of God because God planted the tree for us. God planted a tree on a place called Calvary, a tree that revealed his love and faithfulness to humanity. Christians must remember that we must point a secular and dying world to a tree called Calvary. Kings and kingdoms will all pass away, but only what is done for Christ and his kingdom will last forever.

When George Briggs was governor of Massachusetts, he had three friends who visited Israel. One of the attractions they visited was Golgotha. As they made their way up Calvary's slope, one of the men picked up a branch to help him make the climb. When the men returned from their trip, they gave the governor the stick they had picked up on Calvary and said, "Governor, we want you to know that when we stood on Calvary, we remembered you." He accepted the gift with gratitude and replied to the men, "I appreciate your consideration of me, gentlemen, but I am still more thankful for Christ, who thought of me there."

The greatest difference that Christians can make in our community is to point people to the tree of Calvary. The greatest impact we can have on a community for God is to proclaim the truth of Christ in a world that so desperately needs him. The body of Christ as a whole and individually can make a difference. First, we must earn respect by means of our experience with God. God's presence in our life is an asset. Then we must find common ground to work with the secular, a common ground that does not cause us to compromise our character or our principles. We must remember the ultimate purpose of God's people: to point people to Jesus, who can make all the difference in a community.

CHAPTER XIV:

DEFINING MOMENTS IN THE LIFE OF FAITH

Genesis 22:1–19

Introduction

One of my favorite books is *101 Hymn Stories* by Kenneth W. Osbeck. In it, Osbeck shares the inspiring stories behind many of the hymns we know and cherish. What strikes me about many of these inspirational accounts is that many hymns were written out of defining moments in the life of their authors.

Take for instance the hymn *It is Well With My Soul.* Haratio Spafford wrote this great hymn after he lost his four children in an accident at sea. Frances Havergal wrote many of her hymns out of defining moments in her life. Havergal's hymn *I Gave My Life for Thee* was written after she saw a picture that had been painted by an artist named Sternberg. The painting was a picture of Christ wearing a crown of thorns before Pilate and the Jewish religious leaders. Beneath the painting read the words, "This I have done for thee, what hast thou done for me?" Frances Havergal was so moved by the picture that she swiftly wrote a poem, but when she got home she was not pleased with the words, so she threw them into the fire. The paper did not make it into the fire. It is said to have floated out onto the floor, her father later picked it up and encouraged her to put music to it, which she did.[161]

Defining moments are everywhere we look. We have defining moments in history, one such moment being the cross of Jesus Christ. We have defining moments in the history of the church, the great Reformation being one. We have defining moments in the world of sports. I must admit that I cried when Emmitt Smith of the Dallas Cowboys broke Walter Payton's all-time rushing record. As we look at Genesis 22 we come to another defining moment, a defining moment in the life of Abraham.

Those who have any knowledge of the life of Abraham most likely know what took place in Genesis 22. It is by far a defining moment for Abraham and ultimately the high point of his journey of faith.

When we see and experience defining moments in the life of faith, we notice that these moments come in different forms such as trials, tests, and tasks. Defining moments in the life of faith are moments that God uses in the life of his people for a purpose; often that purpose is to mature us.

In our study of Abraham we have seen many defining moments in his life. The first came from his initial call to the life of faith back in Genesis 11 and 12. Another defining moment came when Abraham was faced with a famine in the land that God had promised him. Then there was the promise of a child and the patience needed to wait on God to act. What is interesting about the defining moments in the life of Abraham is that they consist both of failures and victories. The Lord has a way of turning even our low points into defining moments.

The defining moment in Genesis 22 is definitely a high point in the life of Abraham, but only because Abraham faced the challenge and responded to it in a manner that was pleasing to the

---

[161]Kenneth W. Osbeck, *101 Hymn Stories* (Grand Rapids: Kregel Publishing) 102.

Lord. And just as Abraham was faced with many defining moments in his journey of faith, so are we who have started on our own journey of faith.

Defining moments usually challenge our faith, our trust, and our obedience to the Lord. All God's people will face these tests. When we face those defining moments in our journey of faith, we need to remember that these moments are divine.

Defining Moments in the Life of Faith are Divine

I want you to imagine for a minute where Abraham was in his spiritual journey up to this point. Abraham had been walking with the Lord more than twenty-five years. He had seen the Lord do many great things. He has seen the Lord faithfully protect him even when Abraham's faith faltered. Most importantly, he had seen the Lord provide for him something that he thought he would never have, a son. Abraham and Sarah were able to have a child in their old age. This child would fulfill a promise of God to Abraham and become heir to the promises of God given to Abraham. Abraham was quite comfortable at this time in his life. He lived peacefully in the region with king Abimelech, worshipping and witnessing for his God.

It is almost as if Abraham had arrived in his journey of faith. God had blessed him with land and with son. But what we will notice is that the journey of faith has a final destination and that destination is not experienced this side of heaven. As long as we make our pilgrimage, challenges will come our way, challenges that are our defining moments in our journey on this side of heaven.

We become aware of this truth in Genesis 22:1. "Now it came about after these things…." This points us back to the previous chapters in Genesis to remind us of what has taken place up to this point. It also points us forward to another defining moment in the life of Abraham and reminds us that Abraham is still on his pilgrimage and that the Lord is still developing him as a man of faith. The defining moment about to take place in Abraham's life comes as a divine test in the form of a divine task and is a test of Abraham's faith in the Lord.

The Divine Test

Here's more of verse 1, "Now it came about after these things, that God tested Abraham." The author, who was under the inspiration of the Holy Spirit as he wrote, indicates to the readers that what is taking place in these verses is a test that comes from the very hand of God. The Lord put this truth here for our benefit because if we did not know that this was a divine test of Abraham's faith we might misunderstand what the Lord asked of Abraham. The Lord wants us to know that this is a test, but Abraham does not have a clue. His unawareness makes this a monumental moment in Abraham's journey of faith.

But the Lord lets us know immediately that what took place was orchestrated by the very hand of God. The Hebrew word "nasah" is best translated as our English word "test." Some Bible translations use the word "tempt," but the Hebrew word "nasah" has a different meaning than our English word "tempt." The word "tempt" has the connotation of "enticing one to do wrong," whereas the Hebrew word "nasah" has the idea of testing something or someone for the purpose of proving the quality of that someone or something. In this context "nasah" has the meaning of God testing Abraham for a purpose, to refine Abraham's character so that he may enjoy even closer fellowship with the Lord.[162]

It is very important that we differentiate between test and tempt. One person has rightly summarized the difference when he said, "Satan tempts to destroy, but God tests to strengthen us."[163]

---

[162] Archer, Harris, and Waltke 581.
[163] Waltke 304.

Some defining moments in the life of faith come on account of the failure of our faith. Others God never intended for us to experience, but because of our faltering faith God uses our failures to define us. This is not one of those moments in the life of Abraham.

Divine tests that come from the hand of God come in different forms, but for the most part they come in the form of troubles, trials, and tribulations. The New Testament equivalent that helps us understand these divine tests is found in the epistle of James. "Consider it all joy, my brethren, when you encounter various trials, knowing that the testing of your faith produces endurance. And let endurance have its perfect result, so that you may be perfect and complete, lacking in nothing" (James 1:2–4). Defining moments in the life of faith are divine moments that the Lord has us experience for the purpose of growth. That is exactly what took place with Abraham; God tested Abraham through a divine task.

The Divine Task

The final part of Genesis 22:1 says that the Lord called out to Abraham and he responded, "Here I am." The Lord then gave Abraham the divine task, his divine test. The Lord said to Abraham in verse 2, "Take now your son, your only son, whom you love, Isaac, and go to the land of Moriah and offer him there as a burnt offering on one of the mountains on which I will tell you." As you can see, this divine test of Abraham's faith was also a disturbing task.

Had the Lord not told us from the start that this was a test of Abraham's faith then we might misunderstand what God asked of Abraham. When we realize the implications of what the Lord asked Abraham, we realize that this divine task is, from our human perception, contradictory and illogical. What makes this task contradictory is that the Lord asked Abraham to do something that seems contradictory to the Lord's character. The

Lord abhors human sacrifice in pagan religions elsewhere in the Scriptures; why would he demand it here? We must remember that this is only a test of Abraham's faith, of which Abraham is not aware at this time.

This task that the Lord asks of Abraham also seems illogical from the standpoint of God's promises to Abraham. Two great promises were given to Abraham, the promise of a son and the promise of a land, both of which helped fulfill God's promise to Abraham becoming a great nation. The more important of the two was the promise of son because through Abraham's descendants would come the Savior of the world, Jesus Christ. Seemingly, God was now jeopardizing his own plan of redemption with this task. All of God's plans for Abraham and his descendants are now about to be sacrificed on the altar to God. This seems illogical.

The divine task is a test in the sense that the Lord asked Abraham to do something illogical. But even more telling about the type of test is found in who the Lord was asking Abraham to sacrifice, "Take now your son, your only son, whom you love, Isaac." You will notice that the Lord emphasizes Abraham's son, "your son, your only son." This is a test of commitment and love to the Lord. Abraham could not weasel out of this command by offering up his servant or even offering up his other son Ishmael. He had to offer up the son he had waited twenty-five years to be born. He had to give up the son that his precious wife was able to conceive and give birth to through supernatural means. Even more telling of the type of test is the phrase "whom you love." This reveals that Abraham's defining moment was a divine test concerning his affections and who had first place in his heart.

The defining moment for Abraham was a divine test of whether he loved the blessings more than the one who blesses. Whether he loved the gift more than the giver. The defining moment for Abraham was whether he was willing to give up the blessings of God for God himself. Whether he was willing to follow the Lord when all that was in it for him was the Lord himself.[164]

Defining moments in the life of faith are moments when God pushes us out of our comfort zone to see if our affections are for the blessing rather than for the one who blesses. Our Lord Jesus Christ never hesitated to have those who wanted to follow him count the cost of discipleship. When the rich young ruler asked Jesus how he could have eternal life, Jesus did not hesitate to tell him that he had to sell all he had and give it to the poor and follow him. Jesus, hypothetically speaking, spoke about hating one's own family to be able to be his disciple. Jesus did not mean that we must literally hate our families, but what he did mean is that he must have the preeminent place in our affections. We must be willing to sacrifice and surrender all to follow him.

We need to be careful to limit these divine moments to the spectacular. That is, we should not think of these divine moments only as consisting of a call to the mission field or full-time ministry. Everyday occurrences that come our way, when God calls us to move outside of our comfort zone, can be divine moments. This can come in the form of making a phone call to someone who needs to know Christ and telling him or her how Christ has made a difference in your life. Your divine moment could be a call to teach a Sunday school class or help your church in their visitation program or some other ministry in your church. Our own perceptions and comforts are usually at stake with these divine moments.

In 2002, I experienced one of the roughest years for me in the ministry. What I came to learn was that this was a divine moment in my life. The Lord was testing my affections and seeing where they were placed. For several months I contemplated leaving the ministry. I wanted to get out because I did not want to deal with all the heartache that can come from being a pastor. It was during this time that the Lord was saying to me, "Patrick, I know you love to pastor and preach and you love

---

[164]Walton 519.

the enjoyment that can come from your calling, but will you serve me only when there is joy? Will you serve me only when things are going well? Or will you serve me when things are discouraging? Will you serve me when the only thing in it for you is me?"

Is there a defining moment you are being challenged with? Remember that these defining moments are divine moments orchestrated by the hand of God to mature you in your faith. Defining moments in the life of faith are also deciding moments.

Defining Moments in the Life of Faith Are Deciding Moments

As the Lord dealt with me in my divine moment of testing in 2002, I had to come to a decision. Was I willing to follow the Lord and do as he commanded and called me to do, or was I willing to forsake the Lord so that I could enjoy his blessings but not he who blesses? Defining moments in the life of faith are deciding moments, a time when a decision must be made. And as we will see with Abraham he made a decision to obey the command of God.

Decision to Obey the Command of God

Unmistakably, God shows us Abraham's obedience in Genesis 22:3. "So Abraham arose early in the morning and saddled his donkey, and took two of his young men with him and Isaac his son; and he split wood for the burnt offering, and arose and went to the place of which God had told him."

What amazes me in this verse is the absence of any discussion on the part of Abraham. All we see is swift and certain obedience. This is a great contrast when we compare other occasions in the Bible where God called men to a specific task.

Take for instance the story of Moses. God called him to serve, and Moses made every excuse as to why God should not use him. Gideon's behavior also contrasts Abraham's obedience. When the Lord called Gideon to fight, Gideon did not immediately obey; instead, he insisted twice that God send him a sign.

Abraham of all people knew how to "help God out" in situations such as this. When famine came to the land he helped God out by going to Egypt. When Sarah grew tired of waiting on the promised son, Abraham helped God out by sleeping with Hagar. When Abraham found himself in trouble with Pharaoh and Abimelech he helped the Lord out by deceiving the two kings. In those instances, Abraham was not helping, but disobeying the commands of God. But that is not the case this time. God gave him a command and Abraham did not question, discuss, or offer suggestions. He made no attempt to "help God out," but he submitted in total obedience to the command of God. By Abraham not trying to rationalize his way out of this divine moment, he showed his total affection for the Lord.

How would you respond to such a request? I imagine many of us, myself included, would have rationalized our way out of this divine moment. How many times does God ask us to do minimal things compared to what he asked of Abraham, and we fail to obey. You see, divine moments are deciding moments, moments where we as God's people have to decide whether to obey the command of God.

I was once asked by a colleague in ministry, "If God reveals something to you in the Scriptures are you willing to obey it?" Another way to ask that question would be, "When God sends a divine moment of testing in your life through means of a divine task, are you willing to obey the command of God no matter the cost?" Abraham revealed his willingness to obey the command of God. Abraham's decision to obey the command was founded in his decision to trust the character of God.

Decision to Trust the Character of God

Getting back to Genesis 22, Abraham and Isaac arrived at the place where the Lord commanded them to go. They left behind the servants that went with them and they made their way to the place of sacrifice. On their way, Isaac asked his father an obvious question. "Isaac spoke to his father Abraham and said, 'My father!' and he said 'Here I am, my son.' Behold, the fire and the wood, but where is the lamb for the burnt offering?' " (Genesis 22:7). Isaac carefully observed that his father made sure that everything else was taken care of, but he wondered about the sacrificial animal.

In Abraham's response to Isaac's question we see the foundation for Abraham's obedience to the command of God. "Abraham said, 'God will provide for himself the lamb for the burnt offering, my son' " (Genesis 22:8). Here we witness Abraham's trust in the character of God. Now, this verse does not do justice to what Abraham is trusting in when he makes this statement. But thanks to progressive revelation we learn exactly what he was thinking about from a New Testament writer who revealed that Abraham, "considered that God is able to raise people from the dead" (Hebrews 11:19). Abraham knew God's character and that God was faithful to his word. Therefore, even if the Lord had him sacrifice his son, he believed that the Lord could raise him from the dead. Abraham trusted in the character of God and that was the foundation for his obedience.

Abraham might have thought that the command was contradictory, irrational, and just outrageous, but he made a decision to love the Lord even when all he got out of it was the Lord. He made a decision to obey the Lord, knowing that he could trust in the character of a good and gracious God. Defining moments are deciding moments for the life of faith, and when God's people obey the commands of God and trust in his character, they find that these defining moments are decisive moments in the life of faith.

Defining Moments in the Life of Faith Are Decisive Moments

The obedience and trust of Abraham to this divine moment unfolds in verses 9 through 10. "Then they came to the place of which God had told him; and Abraham built the altar there and arranged the wood, and bound his son Isaac and laid him on the altar, on top of the wood. Abraham stretched out his hand and took the knife to slay his son." All of Abraham's hopes and dreams are about to be slain on the altar, but what happens next reveals that this divine moment was a decisive one. This moment was decisive in three different ways.

Decisive in What It Accomplished

First, it was decisive in what this divine moment accomplished. In verse 11 we are told that the angel of the Lord called out from heaven to Abraham and he responded, "Here I am." In verse 12 the angel said to Abraham, "Do not stretch out your hand against the lad, and do nothing to him; for now I know that you fear God, since you have not withheld your son, your only son, from me."

God tested Abraham, who passed the test with flying colors. At the heart of this divine moment was the matter of whether Abraham feared the Lord. At the heart of this divine moment was the fact that Abraham loved God more than he loved his son. This is a significant moment in the life of faith, that moment when God says, "Do you love me even when there is nothing in it for you?" When those moments come in your life, will they accomplish what the Lord desires?

Decisive in What Was Learned

Second, this divine moment was decisive in what was learned. Notice what took place in verse 13 after the Lord stopped Abraham from sacrificing Isaac. "Then Abraham raised his eyes and looked, and behold, behind him a ram caught in the thicket by his horns; and Abraham went and took the ram and offered him up for a burnt offering in the place of his son. Abraham called the name of that place The LORD Will Provide, as it is said to this day, 'In the mount of the LORD it will be provided.' "

The Lord substituted a ram in the place of Isaac, and Abraham responded to the Lord's faithfulness by naming the place "The LORD Will Provide." In Hebrew it reads "Jehovah Jireh." Abraham had learned the faithfulness of God throughout the years, but never to the degree he experienced in this divine moment after he made the decision to obey the command of God and trust in his character.

Decisive in What God Did

Third, this divine moment was decisive in what God did for Abraham after he provided the ram. In verse 15 we read, "Then the angel of the Lord called to Abraham a second time from heaven, and said, 'By myself I have sworn, declares the Lord, because you have done this thing and have not withheld your son, your only son, indeed I will greatly bless you, and I will greatly multiply your seed.' "

Do you see the result of Abraham's willingness to give up the blessing of God for God? God blessed him. This should dispel the notion that God is our enemy. The life of total surrender to the Lord is a life that God blesses. When we put God before his blessings he blesses. The greatest blessings are found in the life of surrender and sacrifice.

I shared with you earlier how defining moments in the lives of many of our great hymn writers were the sources of their inspiration. Frances Havergal, who wrote the hymn *I Gave My Life for Thee* is probably more known for another hymn that she wrote, *Take My Life and Let It Be*. Havergal was known as the "consecration poet." These two hymns deal with our total sacrifice and surrender to the Lord. When she wrote the words to

Take My Life and Let it Be, Havergal did so after a divine moment in her life. She was led by the Lord to visit a house that was occupied by five people; some of those people were unbelievers and others were believers who had strayed from the Lord. She spent five days with these people praying for them and pleading with them to come to Christ. By the end of her visit, the Lord was faithful to bring those who did not know Christ to him and those who did know Christ back to him. After leaving the house and reflecting upon the faithfulness of God in that situation, she penned these words as a prayer of consecration unto the Lord, "Take my life and let it be, consecrated, Lord, to Thee. Take my hands, and let them move at the impulse of Thy love."[165]

God's people are faced with defining moments every day. We are faced daily with decisions about whether to give our best to the Lord or to save it for ourselves. We are faced every day with the decision to love God more than we love ourselves.

I would be remiss if I did not show you how this chapter of the book of Genesis is a foreshadowing of the sacrifice of Christ on the cross of Calvary. For it was at Calvary that our heavenly Father would not spare his own Son, but would sacrifice him on the cross in our place so that we could have redemption, the forgiveness of sins, through his Son's blood.

Christians, after all that God has done for us, how can we not surrender all and follow him, trusting him to take care of us? What divine moment in your life demands a decision? Will you show your love to the Lord and put him before yourself?

---

[165]Osbeck 239.

CHAPTER XV:

CONCLUSION

Abraham's journey of faith, which we have observed in Genesis 11 through 22, has been an exciting journey to say the least. It has been amazing to see how the Lord worked in Abraham's life. It has been inspiring to witness how Abraham responded to the Lord's work in his life. It has been a blessing to learn crucial lessons for our own journey of faith.

The apostle Paul said in the book of Romans, "For whatever was written in earlier times was written for our instruction, so that through perseverance and the encouragement of Scriptures we might have hope" (v. 15:4). He was referring to the Old Testament when he wrote these words. Our study of the life of Abraham has truly instructed us so that we may keep moving toward our heavenly home.

There seem to be two overriding themes revealed in these chapters of Genesis that will truly be great lessons for the life of faith. First, we learn that the life of faith is nothing apart from the object of faith. The object of the life of faith is none other than Jehovah. The greatest lesson we discover is the faithfulness of our loving God. He is faithful to carry his children even when they go astray. He is faithful to fulfill his word even when his children jeopardize his word. The life of faith is impossible without the faithful object of the life of faith.

The second theme revealed in these chapters is the objectives of the life of faith. Chapter 12 of this book, *Lessons for the Life of Faith*, truly sums up the objectives of the life of faith: rely on the unwavering nature of the promises of God, respond to the requirements of the precepts of God, and remove the impediments to the power of God. The objectives of the life of faith are to trust in the promises of God, obey the precepts of God, and yield to the power of God. If those who are on the journey of faith strive to fulfill those objectives daily, then the journey of faith will sustain the high points more than the low points.

Let us also remember that God is a good God, and even if we fail in those objectives he will never fail in his. We see this time and again in the life of Abraham. We need to strive in our journey to one day hear those heavenly words from our Lord, "Well done!"

Bibliography

Briscoe, Stuart, *Mastering the Old Testament: Genesis*, Dallas: Word Publishing, 1987

Carter, Tom, *2200 Quotations from the Writings of Charles Spurgeon*, Grand Rapids: Baker, 1988

Dyrness, William, *Themes in Old Testament Theology*, Downers Grove: IVP, 1979

Foster, Elon, *6000 Classic Sermon Illustrations*, Grand Rapids: Baker, 1993

Getz, Gene A., *Abraham: Holding Fast the Will of God*, Nashville: Broadman & Holman, 1996

Green, Michael P., *1500 Illustrations for Biblical Preaching*, Grand Rapids: Baker, 1989

Grudem, Wayne, *Systematic Theology*, Grand Rapids: Zondervan, 1994

Hamilton, Victor P., *The Book of Genesis Chapters 1-17(TNIC)*, Grand Rapids: Eerdmans, 1990

________________, *The Book of Genesis Chapters 18-50(TNIC)*, Grand Rapids: Eerdmans, 1995

Harris, Gleason, & Waltke, *Theological Wordbook of the Old Testament*, Chicago: Moody Press, 1980

Hartley, John E., *Genesis (NIBC)*, Peabody: Hendrickson Publishing, 2000

Kidner, Derek, *Genesis (TOTC)*, Downers Grove: IVP, 1967

Morris, Henry M., *The Genesis Record*, Grand Rapids: Baker, 1976

Osbeck, Kenneth W., *101 Hymn Stories*, Grand Rapids: Kregel, 1982

Peterson, Eugene H., *The Message: The Bible in Contemporary Language,* Colorado Springs: Navpress 2002

Phillips, John, *Exploring Genesis*, Grand Rapids: Kregel, 1980

Ross, Allen P., *Creation and Blessing*, Grand Rapids: Baker, 1996

Sailhamer, John H., *The Pentateuch as Narrative*, Grand Rapids: Zondervan, 1992

Swindoll, Charles R., *The Tale of the Tardy Oxcart*, Nashville: Word, 1998

Summer, William T., *3000 Quotations from the Writings of Matthew Henry,* Grand Rapids: Fleming, 1982

Vos, Howard F., *Genesis (EBC)*, Chicago: Moody Press, 1982

Waltke, Bruce K., *Genesis: A Commentary*, Grand Rapids: Zondervan, 2001

Walton, John H.; Matthews Victor H., *The IVP Bible Background Commentary: Genesis -Deuteronomy,* Downers Grove: IVP, 1997

Walton, John H., *The NIV Application Bible Commentary: Genesis,* Grand Rapids: Zondervan, 2001

Wiersbe, Warren W., *Be Obedient: Learning the Secret of Living by Faith,* Colorado Springs: Chariot Victor Publishing, 1991

Zuck, Roy B., *The Speakers Quote Book*, Grand Rapids: Kregel, 1997